THE ELEMENTS OF E-MAIL STYLE

Communicate Effectively via Electronic Mail

David Angell
and Brent Heslop

Addison-Wesley Publishing Company

Reading, Massachusetts ▪ Menlo Park, California ▪ New York
Don Mills, Ontario ▪ Wokingham, England ▪ Amsterdam
Bonn ▪ Sydney ▪ Singapore ▪ Tokyo ▪ Madrid ▪ San Juan
Paris ▪ Seoul ▪ Milan ▪ Mexico City ▪ Taipei

Library of Congress Cataloging-in-Publication Data
Angell, David
     Elements of E-mail style : communicate effectively via electronic mail / David Angell and Brent Heslop.
        p.   cm.
    Includes index.
    ISBN 0-201-62709-4
    1. Electronic mail systems--Handbooks, manuals, etc.   2. Business writing--Handbooks, manuals, etc.   3. Business communication--Handbooks, manuals, etc. I. Heslop, Brent D.   II. Title.
HE6239.E54A53   1993
808'.066651--dc20

                               93-49717
                                 CIP

Sponsoring Editor: Phil Sutherland
Project Editor: Claire Horne
Production Coordinator: Lora Ryan
Cover design: Jean Seal
Set in Meridien and Futura type by Editorial Services of New England, Inc.

1 2 3 4 5 6 7 8 9 - ARM - 98 97 96 95 94
First printing February 1994

Addison-Wesley books are available for bulk purchases by corporations, institutions, and other organizations. For more information please contact the Corporate, Government and Special Sales Department at (617) 944-3700 x2915.

Contents

Chapter 1

Write Right for the E-mail Medium

Chapter 2

Structure Your E-mail for Impact

Chapter 3

Choosing the Right Words

Chapter 4

Tone, Rhythm, Persuasion—and Flame Control   55

Chapter 5

Build Better Sentences   69

Glossary

English and E-mail Jargon

Appendix

Conventions for Posting on the Internet

Index

Acknowledgments

This project was a writer's dream. It let us explore ways to improve our writing and get paid for it. Creating this e-mail-centric writing guide drew on the talents of many special individuals. We are grateful to the following people for their help: Phil Sutherland at Addison-Wesley, who shared our vision of this book from the start; Kimn Neilson and Jenny Kilgore, our grammatical guides, who were instrumental in helping us translate ever-changing English rhetoric into this concise style guide; Claire Horne and Lora Ryan at Addison-Wesley, who oversaw this project from beginning to end; Joanne Angell, Michael Patterson, Dustin Smith, and Jos Marlowe, a talented team of e-mail aficionados, who freely shared their valuable insights and sound advice while reviewing our manuscript; Brian Fudge and Rich White at Portal Communications and Desirree Madison-Briggs at NETCOM, who gave us access to the Internet for this project; Amy Arnold at America Online who let us use America Online; Timothy Campbell, president of Pinnacle Software, for his impressive ASCII art samples.

Read Me First

Strunk and White's *The Elements of Style* was a revolutionary book. It cut the vast tangle of English rhetoric down to a little book of simple, digestible rules that quickly became the writing how-to bible for its time. But times change and so do written communications. In the '90s, electronic mail (e-mail) is emerging as the mainstream form of written communication. This new medium makes different demands on writing style and has its own unique conventions.

A generation raised on Strunk and White learned to write in a leisurely way, employing a writing and editing process that often took hours or days. This simply doesn't work for messages in the e-mail medium, where turnaround times are often measured in minutes. The fast-paced e-mail medium demands a writing style that is clear and concise without sacrificing speed.

The Elements of E-mail Style is the writing guide for the electronic-mail era. It simplifies and summarizes contemporary rules of writing in the e-mail context, so you can quickly improve your e-mail messages on the fly. *The Elements of E-mail Style* explains how to:

- Grasp new e-mail conventions, such as its jargon, etiquette, politics, and privacy issues
- Structure your e-mail messages for impact

- Simplify your e-mail messages by choosing the right words and cutting word fat
- Achieve the right tone and rhythm
- Build better e-mail messages line by line
- Improve and quickly correct your spelling
- Add expression to your e-mail messages by using punctuation and smileys
- Illuminate your e-mail messages by using formatting and special characters

We hope you find this style guide useful. If you have any comments about this guide, we invite you to send us e-mail.

David Angell   Brent Heslop
dangell@shell.portal.com   bheslop@shell.portal.com

Chapter 1

WRITE RIGHT FOR THE E-MAIL MEDIUM

Faster than a speeding letter, cheaper than a phone call, electronic mail is the communication medium of the '90s. The Electronic Mail Association estimates 30 to 50 million people use e-mail, and the number of users is growing at more than 25 percent per year. E-mail is rapidly becoming the dominant form of business communication. As a result, being proficient at writing effective e-mail is becoming an essential work skill. This chapter explains the benefits of e-mail and its impact on everyday communication. We look at the changing makeup of e-mail messages, how to use the 80/20 rule to improve your e-mail style, and the etiquette and politics of the e-mail medium.

BENEFITS OF THE E-MAIL EXPLOSION

The explosive growth of networks, from the small local area network to the global Internet, is ushering in the e-mail era. Legions of businesses and other organizations have adopted e-mail to connect people within as well as outside their organizations. E-mail is rapidly becoming the main channel for moving information, replacing desktop in- and out-boxes with electronic mailboxes. Individuals from all walks of life are recognizing the benefits of e-mail and connecting to the electronic postal system via the Internet and online services such as

CompuServe and America Online. E-mail is such an elegantly simple idea that once you begin to use it, you wonder how you lived without it. Communicating via e-mail has many advantages.

- E-mail eliminates phone tag. A good number of telephone calls are unsuccessful because their recipients are busy or away. E-mail eliminates this problem, improves response times, and cuts telephone charges in the bargain. E-mail allows you to digest your messages and put more thought into your responses, which you might not be able to do on the phone.
- E-mail breaks down the distance and time barriers of telephone calls and traditional written communication. It lets you send and read e-mail messages at any time, 24 hours a day, 365 days a year, for better communication across time zones.
- E-mail shortens the cycle of written communication. It enables people to circumvent many of the inefficiencies of the office place and the approval process of traditional paper-based communications.
- E-mail empowers individuals by flattening out corporate and sociological hierarchies and allowing for more direct interactive communication.
- E-mail improves productivity in a wide range of interactive activities. It speeds up the decision-making process by providing a forum for replies or clarifications. It also facilitates meeting planning and preparation.
- E-mail creates flexibility in the workday by reducing telephone interruptions. It also allows people to work at home or at any location with a computer.

THE CHANGING E-MAIL MESSAGE

E-mail correspondence is evolving from the freewheeling short, chatty e-mail messages of early technical users to the more sophisticated documents used by business today. As more business communication moves over to e-mail, the need for better e-mail writing techniques increases. Yet many early e-mail users and pundits, such as Macintosh evangelist Guy Kawasaki, maintain you should not add stylistic and grammatical refinements to your e-mail messages because they'll slow you down. In his book, *The Guy Kawasaki Computer Curmudgeon* (Hayden Books, 1992), Kawasaki sums up this perspective by telling the e-mail communicator to "ignore stylistic and grammatical considerations."

> Using e-mail saves time because careful editing and proofing are not necessary or appropriate. E-mail is supposed to be fast, tit-for-tat communication. You ask. I answer. You ask. I answer. You're not supposed to watch the sun set, listen to the surf pound the sun-bleached sand, and sip San Miguel beer as Paco dives for abalone while you craft your e-mail.

It is true that e-mail is often written on the fly without time for leisurely editing and proofing. It is also true that if you try to improve your e-mail writing using the traditional approach of paper-based communication, you dilute the power of the e-mail medium. Conventional paper-based business communications, such as letters and memos, take hours or days from first draft to final delivery. This simply doesn't work with messages in the fast-paced e-mail environment, where turnaround times are often measured in minutes.

Developing an e-mail writing style that is effective and timely requires an e-mail-centric approach to writing. E-mail is not merely the bastard child of the print medium; it has its own needs and conventions, its own strengths and weaknesses. Consequently, many questions of style, long ago settled for print media and fixed into rules of style manuals, need to be reexamined in light of the new e-mail medium.

USE THE 80/20 RULE TO IMPROVE YOUR E-MAIL STYLE

The 80/20 rule is a principle developed by Vilfredo Pareto, an Italian mathematician and economist. The rule states that, in any process or task, 80 percent of the problems are a result of 20 percent of the causes. The 80/20 rule is a strategy you can use to improve your e-mail writing. By focusing on the 20 percent of English grammar, usage, and mechanics issues that cause 80 percent of the problems in writing e-mail, you can quickly and dramatically improve your e-mail messages. In other words, focusing on the right mix of essential e-mail writing techniques within the e-mail context allows you to develop an effective, on-the-fly e-mail writing style.

E-MAIL ETIQUETTE AND POLITICS

The instantaneous, spontaneous nature of e-mail has inherent dangers. The computer screen is impersonal and makes it easy to be blunt. People feel freer when communicating through e-mail than they do face to face. This lack of inhibition is a double-edged sword; it can be useful for collaboration, but it can also be destructive. The e-mail medium is fertile ground for misunderstandings and unintended hurt feelings. Etiquette and politics are important factors to keep in mind as you write your e-mail messages.

Don't Flame

In the lingo of e-mail, a **flame** is an inflammatory remark or message. Sending messages that contain insensitive language or impetuous negative responses is called **flaming**. Emotions and tempers can flare in e-mail communication just as quickly as a flame ignites. You disagree with someone, so you fire back a quick retort.

The person at the other end takes offense and sends back an angry message. The result is a **flame war** or **flame-fest**, two or more people firing angry messages back and forth in what is the equivalent of an online food fight. Flaming is even more common in public forums such as newsgroups on the Internet, where messages are subject to little accountability. See the Appendix for more information on the dos and don'ts of posting messages on the Internet. Here are guidelines to help you keep flaming under control.

- Before you send an e-mail message, ask yourself, Would I say this to the person's face?

- Wait until you have a chance to calm down before responding to an offensive message. Like slipping a letter through the mail slot in a post office box, once you send an e-mail message, you are committed to it.

- Read your message twice before you send it and check to make sure you didn't write anything that might be misinterpreted.

- Don't use abusive or obscene language in e-mail.

- Don't assume every outrageous message is a flame. Flaming isn't always a fighting match. If you think that a message is totally outrageous, it might be a joke waiting for you to add the punch line.

- Avoid flaming in public forums. If you disagree, respond to the originator of a message directly. Others often do not appreciate or want to participate in your debate.

- Indicate to the recipient that you are knowingly blowing off steam when you flame by constructing your message as follows:

```
Flame On:
```

message text

```
Flame Off.
```

Note: Chapter 4 explains techniques for changing a negative message to a positive message, and other ways to
combat flaming.

Respect E-mail Confidentiality

Accessing other people's e-mail without their specific
permission is an intrusion of privacy. The ease with
which this is accomplished in no way justifies it. Here are
two common-sense rules for respecting the e-mail confidentiality of others.

- Don't read printed e-mail messages waiting to be
  picked up from a printer; they are considered confidential material.

- Ask for permission before forwarding, inserting, or
  posting someone else's e-mail message; it might cause
  embarrassment or confidentiality problems for the
  author of the message.

Watch What You Say in E-mail

Chances are Big Brother is watching you. The 1986
Electronic Communications Privacy Act (ECPA) prohibits
phone and dataline taps with two exceptions: law-
enforcement agencies and *employers*. This act considers
internal e-mail to be the property of the company that
pays for the e-mail system. Therefore companies have
the right to search their company mailboxes. Results of a
survey in *MacWorld* magazine (July 1993) should end
any feelings of privacy you might have had about your
e-mail. Of the respondents that said they electronically
eavesdrop on employees, 41 percent said e-mail was
inspected, and nearly two-thirds of management sur-
veyed maintained that they were justified in monitoring
electronic communications.

If you're concerned about the privacy of your e-mail,
find out if the company you work for has a policy regarding its employees' e-mail. Until the final verdict on the

privacy of e-mail is in, the best defense against anyone reading your messages is to watch what you write.

Protect Yourself against E-mail Break-ins

When you leave your computer unattended, make sure your e-mail program can't be used by someone else while you're away. If an unauthorized person gains access to your e-mail account, worse things can happen than just having your messages looked at, modified, or deleted. Your e-mail account can be used to send or post offensive messages, the results of which can be devastating. Many systems let you lock your screen to prevent anyone from using your system. Unlocking the screen requires a password. Here are some tips for keeping out unauthorized users.

- Never give your e-mail user name and password to someone else.
- Be careful of anyone claiming by phone or e-mail to be a system administrator asking for your password. This could be a ruse to get privileged information the way con artists try to get your credit card number over the phone.

Be Careful about Copyrights and Licenses

It's perfectly legal to reproduce short extracts of a copyrighted work to pass along to others, but complete reproduction of a copyrighted work is strictly and explicitly forbidden by United States law and by the international copyright law of fair use. "Fair use" is a deliberately ambiguous term. Quoting a long passage from a lengthy book might be acceptable, but quoting the same amount of text from a short book would not. Here are some guidelines for using copyrighted material in an e-mail message.

- Don't quote more than a few contiguous paragraphs or stanzas at a time. Make sure that quotations, even if scattered, don't overshadow your message.

- State where your facts come from when using facts to support your case.

- Don't take someone else's ideas and use them as your own. You don't want someone pretending that your ideas are theirs; show them the same respect.

Eliminate Sexist Language from Your E-mail

A big shift in business and personal communication is a recognition of the way language reflects our attitude toward the equality of the sexes. Sexist masculine pronouns and gender-specific titles are rooted in our language like weeds. In order to achieve nonsexist language in your communications, become sensitive to the ways traditional wording treats gender. Consider your reader's reaction to the language you use. The following pointers can prevent you from excluding or offending a reader.

- Use the same treatment for men's and women's names. If you use a man's first and last name, use a woman's first and last name.

- If you use the courtesy title Mr. for men, then use Ms. for women. A woman's marital status should not be identified by the courtesy title.

Eliminate Masculine Pronouns   Historically, our language has used masculine pronouns *(he, his, him, himself)* to refer to both sexes. But in the last few decades, it has become widely acknowledged that using only masculine nouns and pronouns or referring to women in terms that are different from those used for men implies a sexist attitude. The English language provides a variety of useful alternatives; however, no single technique works in all situations. Here are several ways to avoid the pronoun *he* in the sentence *When a collector buys The Best of Burl Ives, he receives a life-size, porcelain Burl Ives statue.*

- Eliminate the gender-specific pronoun and use a relative pronoun. *A collector who buys The Best of Burl Ives receives a life-size, porcelain Burl Ives statue.*

- Rewrite a statement in the plural form. *When collectors buy The Best of Burl Ives, they receive a life-size, porcelain Burl Ives statue.*

- Use *you.* Don't, however, shift back and forth between *you* and *he or she. When you buy The Best of Burl Ives, you receive a life-size, porcelain statue of Burl Ives.*

- Use a participial phrase. A participial phrase is a group of words containing a verb ending with *-ing* or *-ed* that acts as an adjective. *A collector buying The Best of Burl Ives receives a life-size, porcelain Burl Ives statue.*

- Repeat the noun. *When a collector buys The Best of Burl Ives, the collector receives a life-size, porcelain Burl Ives statue.*

- Rephrase the sentence to change the subject and avoid using a gender-specific pronoun. *A life-size, porcelain Burl Ives statue accompanies every purchase of The Best of Burl Ives.*

- Rewrite the sentence using the passive voice. *When a collector buys The Best of Burl Ives, a life-size, porcelain Burl Ives statue is included in the purchase.*

- Use *he or she.* Keep in mind that overusing this form can be distracting. *When a collector buys the Best of Burl Ives, he or she receives a life-size, porcelain Burl Ives statue.*

Avoid Gender-specific Titles   Certain job titles indicate the sex of the person—for example, waitress and actress. Many other titles, such as journalist and author, do not. In the last several years, occupational titles have become more gender-neutral. *Men Working* signs now read *Road Work.* The following are examples of gender-specific job titles and their non-gender-specific equivalents.

**Table 1.1 Commonly used gender-specific words
and their alternatives**

Gender-specific Title	Alternative
airline stewardess	flight attendant
chairman	chairperson or chair
delivery boy	deliverer, messenger
fireman	fire fighter
foreman	supervisor
man-hours	work-hours, person-hours
mankind	humanity, humankind
newsman	reporter, journalist
policeman, policewoman	police officer
postman	letter carrier, mail carrier
repairman	service technician, repair person
salesman	sales representative
self-made man	self-made person
spokesman	spokesperson
workman	worker

Be Culturally Aware for International E-mail

E-mail knows no geographical boundaries. A message can be sent as easily to an office down the hall or an office across the globe. When communicating with individuals of other cultures, be aware of cultural differences in perceptions and norms. Here are some tips to help you be more sensitive to cultural differences.

- Give metric measurements, followed by English-system equivalents. *Do you know where I can get my hands on 29.6 milliliters (1 fluid ounce) of nitroglycerin for my nephew's science project?*
- Inform the reader what format (for dates, times, and numbers) or system (monetary) you're using. Americans read the date 7/8/94 as July 8, 1994; Europeans

read it as August 7, 1994. The Japanese often format dates in year/month/day order. Europeans use a 24-hour clock.

- Use generic terms instead of trademarks. *Someone spilled a Mountain Dew and destroyed our Xerox machine, so I'm sending you the original file* should read *Someone spilled a soft drink and destroyed our photocopy machine, so I'm sending you the original file.*

- Use a definite reference when referring to a geographical region. In the following sentence, someone in another country may ascribe a different locale to the *east coast* reference. *The amnesiacs' convention is taking place on the east coast, but I can't remember the date.* Instead, write *The amnesiacs' convention is taking place in New York City, but I can't remember the date.*

- Avoid humor and sarcasm—they don't travel easily across cultures.

- Don't say *no* directly to an offer made by a Japanese person; it's considered impolite. The Japanese also consider it impolite to display anger.

- Be aware that not all speakers of the same language are culturally the same. For example, cultural differences exist among French speakers in Canada, Switzerland, and France, just as cultural differences exist among English speakers in the United States, England, and Australia.

Avoid Using All Capital Letters

Typing your message all in upper-case letters is known in the world of e-mail as **shouting**. Using all caps means you don't need to use the Shift key repeatedly (you just turn on Caps Lock), but what is easier for you becomes a burden for the recipient reading the message. A message written in upper-case letters is difficult to read. All caps are much harder to read because people recognize words not only by their letter groups, but also by their shapes.

When a word is all caps, you have to read it letter by letter, rather than subconsciously recognizing groups of letters. Compare the two following examples (overlooking Woody Allen's use of the sexist noun "mankind").

MORE THAN ANY TIME IN HISTORY MANKIND FACES A CROSSROADS. ONE PATH LEADS TO DESPAIR AND UTTER HOPELESSNESS, THE OTHER TO TOTAL EXTINCTION. LET US PRAY THAT WE HAVE THE WISDOM TO CHOOSE CORRECTLY. — WOODY ALLEN

More than any time in history mankind faces a crossroads. One path leads to despair and utter hopelessness, the other to total extinction. Let us pray that we have the wisdom to choose correctly. — Woody Allen

Avoid Using All Lower-case Letters

Like a message in all upper-case letters, a message in all lower-case letters is easier for the sender to type but harder for the recipient to read. It's much easier to read a mixture of upper-case and lower-case letters than to read text that contains only lower-case letters. Using all lower-case letters is annoying for the recipient and can result in your message being misunderstood or not read at all. Compare the following example with the previous one.

more than any time in history mankind faces a crossroads. one path leads to despair and utter hopelessness, the other to total extinction. let us pray that we have the wisdom to choose correctly. — woody allen

Check Your E-mail Regularly

If you don't check your electronic mailbox or **inbox** regularly, you sabotage the advantages e-mail has over the U.S. postal system (known as **snail-mail** among most e-mail users). People who read their e-mail only once a week defeat the purpose of having an e-mail system. Of course, you can go overboard checking your mail. Responding to mail a few times a day is more efficient than checking and responding to mail as it comes in. A good routine is to check for mail in the morning, at lunchtime, and before you leave for the day. Many e-mail systems automatically notify you with a beep when you have new mail, so you don't need to do a manual check.

When Not to Use E-mail

E-mail is convenient, saves time, and cuts down on playing phone tag, but it's not a perfect communication vehicle. It sacrifices several of the interpersonal aspects of communication: facial expression, body language, and voice intonation. In e-mail there is also a longer lag time for responses and clarifications than there is in phone communication. If the message is very important, controversial, or confidential, or if it could be easily misunderstood, think twice about sending it by way of e-mail and consider the telephone or a face-to-face meeting.

Chapter 2

STRUCTURE YOUR E-MAIL FOR IMPACT

Elmore Leonard, writer of best-selling mystery and suspense fiction, once stated, "I try to leave out the parts that people skip." This is good advice for structuring your e-mail messages. Communications for the e-mail medium should be structured in a way that is radically different from traditional paper-based business communications. The fast pace of reading and writing e-mail on computers affects what you should and should not include in your messages. This chapter lays out a blueprint of the elements you can use to structure your e-mail messages for maximum impact.

ANATOMY OF AN E-MAIL MESSAGE

While different e-mail systems provide different interfaces and features, the essential compositional elements of an e-mail message are standardized. The typical e-mail message is made up of a few key components: the `To`, `Cc`, `Bcc`, `Subject`, and `Attachment` lines make up what is referred to as the **header** of an e-mail message, while the message text area is called the **body** of a message. Figure 2.1 shows a sample e-mail message. Table 2.1 describes each element of a typical e-mail message.

FIGURE 2.1

A typical e-mail
message

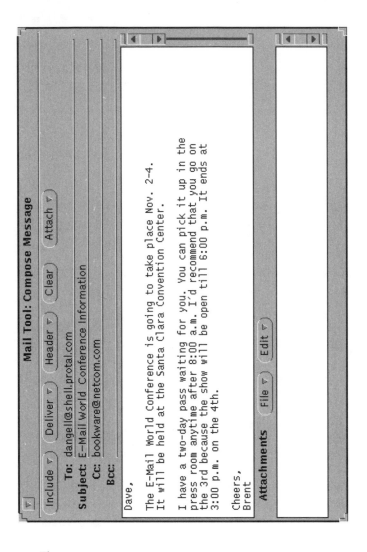

```
                    Mail Tool: Compose Message
 (Include ▽) (Deliver ▽) (Header ▽) (Clear) (Attach ▽)

      To: dangell@shell.protal.com
 Subject: E-Mail World Conference Information
      Cc: bookware@netcom.com
     Bcc:

 Dave,

 The E-Mail World Conference is going to take place Nov. 2-4.
 It will be held at the Santa Clara Convention Center.

 I have a two-day pass waiting for you. You can pick it up in the
 press room anytime after 8:00 a.m. I'd recommend that you go on
 the 3rd because the show will be open till 6:00 p.m. It ends at
 3:00 p.m. on the 4th.

 Cheers,
 Brent

 Attachments  (File ▽)  (Edit ▽)
```

Table 2.1 Elements of an e-mail message

E-mail Message Element	Description
To	The **To line** is the place to enter e-mail addresses.
Cc	The **Cc line** (*Cc* stands for carbon copy or courtesy copy) is the place to enter e-mail addresses of people to whom you want to send a copy of the message.
Bcc	The **Bcc line** (*Bcc* stands for blind carbon copy) line lets you specify e-mail addresses of people to whom you want to send copies of a message without the original recipient's knowledge.
Subject	The **Subject line** is the place to enter a short description of the e-mail message. The subject line appears in the recipient's inbox listing of messages.
Attachments	The **attachments** line or area allows you to enter the name of a file or drag and drop an icon representing a file to attach it to your e-mail message.
Message text area	The **message text area** contains the body of your e-mail message. Common text-editing features such as cut, copy, and paste are usually available for writing messages.

HOW AND WHEN TO USE To, Cc, Bcc, AND RECEIPTS

Because it's so easy, it's tempting to send carbon copies or blind carbon copies routinely. Likewise, regularly using

receipts might seem like a good idea. **Receipts** are messages an e-mail system generates to inform the sender
that recipients have received the message sent to them.
Just because a feature is easy to use, however, doesn't
mean it should be used frequently. Here are some pointers
for using mail header features and receipts.

- Send carbon copies of messages only to those who
  need a copy. Sending unnecessary carbon copies
  wastes everyone's time.

- Be careful with blind carbon copies. They can be dan-
  gerous if you accidentally send them to the wrong
  people. Blind carbon copies can imply that you are
  going behind someone's back.

- Avoid using receipts, which can easily be interpreted
  as insulting. In most cases, you're saying to the recipient, "You never read your e-mail, so I asked for a
  receipt. Now I know you received it and you don't
  have an excuse not to answer." In some cases, however, a receipt provides an audit trail for clarifying
  routing problems or for settling disputes.

- Put addresses in the To, Cc, and Bcc lines in alphabetical order of the recipients' last names. This keeps
  you from inadvertently alienating managers or
  coworkers by listing them in the wrong place.

> **Note:**   Most e-mail systems let you create an **alias,** which
> is a name that specifies a group of e-mail addresses. By
> simply typing the alias name in the To, Cc, or Bcc lines,
> you automatically add all the e-mail addresses stored in the
> alias.

HOW TO SURVIVE E-MAIL TRIAGE

Volumes of e-mail arrive in electronic mailboxes every
day. To get through these messages, people scan them to
see who they are from and what the subject matter is in
order to decide which messages deserve their attention.

If they get beyond the subject line, they scan the first screenful of the message. Scanning these two parts of an e-mail message is the basis of e-mail triage. Messages that don't attract the reader at these fundamental points of reference run the risk of not getting read or of being deleted.

> **Note:** A growing number of e-mail users employ e-mail **filters** to save them from drowning in a sea of messages. These utility programs let you automatically sort your incoming mail into a priority system according to various criteria, such as who the sender is or certain key words in the subject line or message text. For example, you can set it up so that messages from your boss become first priority—or last, depending on your attitude.

Make the Subject Line Compelling

The subject line is the first thing the recipient of your e-mail sees. A concise and informative subject line can prompt a recipient to read your message. The subject line is listed in the recipient's inbox, along with subject lines from other e-mail messages. The following guidelines will help you make the biggest impact with your subject line.

- Write the important points in the first half of your subject line. Subject lines are often truncated in a recipient's inbox listing. The first 25 to 35 characters of a subject line are usually displayed.

- Phrase a subject line so that it tells the reader what to do, instead of, or in addition to, what your message is about. For example, the subject line *Send guidelines for donut day* gets the main message across in the subject line.

- Don't use wild, attention-grabbing statements just to get your message read. For example, when the messages prove to be less than urgent, using *URGENT* in your subject line too many times reduces the value of urgency in the recipient's mind.

- Make it clear in the subject line if the message is being sent to a group. For example, you might enter *Schedule for bowling league members.*

Make a Good First Screen Impression

How information is presented in the first screenful of a message is an important part of communicating via e-mail. Whether the recipient reads past the first screenful of information can depend on how you present your information. Most e-mail messages are less than three paragraphs in length and fit into this first screen. However, an increasing number of multi-page documents— newsletters, proposals, reports, and forms—are being sent via e-mail. Even these messages can be presented in ways that make an impact in the first screen, as explained later in this chapter.

> **Note:** For information on formatting techniques to make your messages more attractive, such as emphasizing text, creating headlines, drawing boxes, and other pointers, see Chapter 8.

Keep Your Reader's Terminal in Mind

If you're sending an e-mail message to someone who is using a computer or an e-mail system that is different from yours, keep in mind they're not all created equal. If you're using a terminal that displays 100 characters on a line, for example, remember that many e-mail readers have an 80-character terminal. A message that wraps incorrectly slows down and irritates the reader. Here are some guidelines for sending e-mail messages that can be read on different types of terminals or e-mail systems.

- Press Enter at the point you want each line to end. Even though a sentence wraps on your screen, it's not considered a line until you press Enter.

- Keep your line length less than 80 characters. On some terminals the lines might not wrap at all and the last 20 characters of a 100-character line will not be displayed.

- Keep the line length to less than 60 characters if your message is likely to be forwarded. Forwarded messages are often indented by a tab character, which is usually 8 characters in length.

- Don't use font features, such as boldface and italics, unless you're sure the recipient's computer and e-mail system are capable of reproducing these effects. When you use formatting features, a string of control characters is sent that can create problems on different systems.

HOW TO SHAPE YOUR MESSAGE

Shape your e-mail message so that it has a structure that is easy to follow. This is crucial to communicating your points quickly. Not addressing your reader, randomly presenting topics, or disregarding structural enhancements are all factors that slow down the reader trying to make sense of your message. The following sections explain how to construct your e-mail to deliver your message efficiently.

Add a Greeting for a Friendly Touch

Just because e-mail is for quick communication shouldn't prevent you from taking a moment to add a friendly touch. It's true that the receiver can see in the header who the message is from, but adding a greeting at the beginning of your message body makes it more personal. Of course, a greeting is inappropriate for an e-mail message to a public forum. Here are guidelines for adding greetings to your messages.

- Start the message with the person's first name if you're communicating with a person you know on that basis.

- Identify yourself appropriately in the first few lines after your greeting if you're sending a message to someone who doesn't know you. It might be beneficial to let your reader know what department or company you work for or who referred you to him or her.

- Use a friendly generic greeting, such as *Greetings*, when sending a message to a group of people with whom you regularly communicate.

- Don't use outdated or gender-specific forms, such as *Dear Sirs* or *Gentlemen*, from traditional business correspondence.

- Be aware that greetings tend to be more formal and traditional in some parts of the world, such as Japan and Europe. See Chapter 1 for information on cultural awareness in e-mail communication.

Write from the Top Down

Writing a message from the top down, also called the *inverted-pyramid* writing method, is a technique used by newspaper reporters. Each inch of an inverted-pyramid story is less important than the inch that precedes it. When a five-inch story needs to fit into a four-inch space, the newspaper editor simply cuts an inch off the bottom rather than running through the story looking for expendable words or sentences. Newspapers use the inverted-pyramid method because they're in the business of delivering facts to readers as quickly as possible in tightly defined spaces. A reporter puts the who, what, when, where, and why in the first paragraph and develops the supporting information under it. Writing your e-mail messages using the inverted-pyramid method gets your point across in the first screenful.

Put Yourself in the Recipient's Shoes

Readers are motivated by their needs and interests. For the best results, put what your reader wants to hear above what you want to say. Organize your thoughts according to the way your reader thinks about the subject. Keep in mind that the reader wants the results of your thinking, not the thinking itself. You can't be a mind reader, but asking yourself some pointed questions about your objective and about your reader will help you decide on the length, scope, content, structure, development, style, and tone of your message. Of course, not every message needs this much thought. For those that do, take the time to answer the following questions to make your messages more concrete.

- What is the purpose of the message? Am I writing to inquire, inform, persuade, or motivate, or do I have more than one purpose?

- What is the content of the message? What kinds of information will help me achieve my purpose? Do I have all the information I need?

- How interested or involved or knowledgeable is my reader regarding the subject? Given my needs and my reader's needs, how much information should I include?

- What is my reader's purpose for reading? To make a decision? To be better informed?

- Does my reader have special concerns or strong views about the subject? What are they?

- How does my reader regard me personally and professionally?

- What is my reader's style of doing business?

- What are the constraints I'm dealing with? What can work against me or make my task more difficult?

- What is the reader's skill level and experience with e-mail?

Note: See Chapter 4 for more information on how to write persuasive messages.

Make Responding Easy

E-mail messages frequently are quick exchanges—you ask your question and get your answer. Recipients of e-mail messages reply more expeditiously to messages that clearly state the type of response needed. Here are some guidelines that will improve your chances of getting the response you need.

- Make sure you provide enough information so the recipient can respond. If the recipient doesn't have enough information to give an answer, you'll end up bouncing messages back and forth just to clarify points.
- Phrase a message so that the reader can reply with a yes or no answer or a short response. For example, use questions instead of statements. Instead of writing *Let me know your thoughts on Joanne's proposal for disco bowling*, write *Should we adopt Joanne's proposal for disco bowling?*
- Ask for a reply at the beginning of your message or even in the subject line.

Develop Focused Paragraphs

Paragraphs—groups of related sentences—are the basic building blocks of writing. The main point of a paragraph should be stated at the beginning, in the topic sentence, with each following sentence contributing to the main topic. A paragraph usually contains more than one point, but the points should all relate to the main topic. Here are the key components of a focused paragraph.

- Use a strong topic sentence that draws the reader in to the paragraph.
- Make sure that every sentence in the paragraph contributes to the topic by explaining, expanding, illustrating, or proving it.
- Include in the paragraph all the information needed to address the topic completely.

- Omit any sentences that don't relate directly to the topic of the paragraph.

Use Short Paragraphs

Readers are turned off by large chunks of text. Information is absorbed more easily when it is presented in short, coherent units. Short paragraphs allow the reader mentally to take a breath between weighty chunks of thought. Using short paragraphs not only avoids overwhelming the reader, but also provides relief to the reader's eye, making the message more readable. Readability should override the sometimes conflicting goal of continuity. Of course, breaking a long paragraph into smaller ones doesn't solve problems of wordiness or poor organization. Here are some pointers to help you keep your paragraphs short, sweet, and easily delineated.

- If a paragraph contains too many separate ideas, break it into a bulleted or numbered list.
- If a paragraph is short, don't add unrelated information to fill it out. Leave it short.
- Split up a paragraph that is too long to be read comfortably, even if it is one logical unit.
- Use double line spacing between paragraphs. The additional space makes it easier to read the screen (or a printout, if your reader decides to print the message). Avoid indenting paragraphs. This is unnecessary if you insert extra space between paragraphs.

Lists Deliver Information Efficiently

One of the most effective ways to structure information in e-mail messages is to use bulleted or numbered lists. Lists add clarity and improve the visual impact of a page. They set off multiple items so that your reader can easily follow your points. In a bulleted list, all items have equal emphasis. In a numbered list, the items form a sequence with a number or letter to identify each item. Here are general rules for writing lists.

- Capitalize the first word of a list item and, if it's a sentence, end it with a period.
- Use either sentences or fragments. Don't mix them in the same list.
- Keep list items parallel in form. The following example lists the favorite pastimes of dogs in nonparallel and parallel form.

  Not parallel: *Getting treats, hide the bone, sniff the neighbor, dog poetry.*

  Parallel: *Getting treats, hiding the bone, sniffing the neighbor, reciting dog poetry.*

- Keep list items about the same length, if possible.
- If you use an incomplete sentence to introduce a list, don't continue it after the list.
- You can terminate the sentence that introduces a list with a colon if the words *as follows* or *the following* are used.
- Separate the bullet or number from the text with a tab space, not spacebar spaces, to ensure that your text lines up properly.

Emphasize Key Points with Bullets   A bulleted list helps the reader focus quickly on key points. Bulleted lists are used to present lists of parallel items without emphasizing sequence. There is no one standard bullet character that can be displayed on all computer systems. Therefore, when you create a bulleted list in an e-mail message, you need to use a stand-in character. Two popular bullet alternatives are the asterisk followed by a tab space, and the dash followed by a tab space. Here is an example of asterisks used as bullets in a list.

```
  * Use bullets sparingly so that they don't lose
    their impact.
```

```
* Maintain parallelism in bulleted lists.
* Begin each point with a capital letter.
* Use either sentences or fragments, but don't
  mix them in the same list.
* Make sure all the items have equal emphasis.
* Keep bulleted list items roughly the same
  length.
```

Use Numbered Lists for Sequential Items   Numbered lists imply the importance of sequence in the points you want to make. Numbering or lettering a list lets your readers follow the sequence more easily. Here is an example of a numbered list.

```
1. Choose the Compose button.
2. Type the e-mail address of the recipient in
   the To line.
3. Move to the Cc line and type the e-mail
   address if you want to send a carbon copy.
4. Type the subject of your message in the
   Subject line.
5. Move to the message body and type your
   message.
6. Choose the Send button.
```

Save Space with Embedded Lists   An embedded list presents items in paragraph form. You can use an embedded list as a stand-alone paragraph or within a paragraph. An embedded list takes up less screen space and can help you keep your most important points within a paragraph or the first screenful. (You do, however, sacrifice some of the clarity of bulleted and numbered lists.)

Here is an example of an embedded list.

```
Embedded lists must be (1) located within a
paragraph, (2) used for short items, and (3)
punctuated like a sentence.
```

Here are some guidelines for creating an embedded list.

- Be sure all the list items are short.
- Punctuate the list items as you would any sentence.
- Identify each item with a number or letter in parentheses.
- Begin each item (except proper nouns) with a lower-case letter.

How to Structure a Long Message

E-mail messages come in all sizes. If you're sending an e-mail message that is longer than a few screenfuls, take special care to keep the reader interested. Here are some tips for creating long messages.

- In the first screen of your message, include a table of contents that covers the important points of your message.
- If you need to solicit a response from the recipient, do it in the first screen.
- Include an executive summary of your message in the first screen. An **executive summary** is a short paragraph or section that precedes a lengthy document and highlights its key points. It is designed for people who don't have the time to read the full text, but need to know what the document contains.
- Use white space and other graphic devices, such as lines composed of hyphens or asterisks, to enhance message readability. See Chapter 8 for information on formatting options that can enhance your e-mail messages.

Headings Break Up Long Messages   In e-mail messages longer than a few screenfuls, use headings to guide your reader through the material. Headings break the text into sections, making the material easier to digest. They also provide quick reference points to help the reader find specific information without reading the entire document. Here are some pointers for using headings.

- Identify each section of your e-mail message with a heading that indicates the key concept or major thought of the section.
- Use headings that are either brief and to the point or longer and more descriptive—your choice will depend on the audience—but don't mix them.
- Don't make your headings so terse that they don't have any meaning.
- Keep headings parallel. Avoid combining headings like *Understanding Cartoon Laws of Physics* and *Flubber Physics*. Instead, keep them parallel: *Cartoon Laws of Physics* and *Flubber Physics*.
- Use double line spacing before and after a heading to add visual emphasis.

How to Reply to an E-mail Message

E-mail systems let you reply to a message directly from your inbox with the press of a key or the click of a mouse. The reply feature automatically addresses the e-mail message to the person who sent the original message and adds the subject line of the original message in the reply message's subject line. Most systems also let you insert the text of the original message into your reply message. To make the inserted text stand out from your reply, many e-mail systems begin each line of the original message with a special character, such as a greater-than sign (>) or a colon (:). Here are some guidelines for structuring replies to e-mail messages.

- Edit the original message to include only enough information to remind the sender of his or her original question or purpose. If the original message is long, you can place it below your reply message.

- Don't repeat the original message if it's a simple request and you're sure the recipient will know what you're responding to, but remember that many e-mail users send and receive volumes of e-mail and can easily forget what they've requested.

- Some e-mail systems support a reply-all feature, which sends your reply to everyone listed in the To or Cc lines of the original message. Be careful not to use this feature if your message is personal or if you don't want your reply to be read by anyone but the sender.

- Don't leave the sender of an e-mail message hanging; slow replies negate the benefits of e-mail. If you don't have a full answer to an e-mail inquiry and need some extra time, send a quick message to let the sender know you have read the message and intend to reply.

- If you are forwarding a message to another person, include an explanation if the receiver will be confused by the message's contents. You can edit out any extraneous material from a message you're forwarding.

- Don't modify the subject line if you're sending a reply to a recipient who is using an e-mail filter program, because many filters require an exact match to the original text string.

Include a Simple Closing

A long-winded closing can water down a strong message. An e-mail message closing usually includes a simple closing statement, then your name or initials. Many e-mail writers like to close with just their name or initials. When writing a closing, use these guidelines.

- Don't use closings that are carryovers from the old-fashioned business letter. Avoid *Sincerely yours* or *If you have any questions, please call (or e-mail)*.

- Use simple closings, such as *Thanks* or *Regards*. Many e-mail users like to close with an abbreviated expression, such as *THX* (thanks) or *TTFN* (ta ta for now). Chapter 6 includes a table of commonly used abbreviations.

- Be careful with closings in international e-mail. If you are writing to someone in Europe or Japan, for example, you might need to use a more formal and traditional closing. Chapter 1 discusses issues you should be aware of in writing international e-mail.

- Put one or two hyphens before your name on a separate line to set it off from the text of your message.

> **Note:** Many e-mail systems let you add a signature file to the end of your e-mail message. A **signature file** is a text file containing additional information about you that is inserted at the bottom of your e-mail messages. See Chapter 8 for more information on creating and using a signature file.

When to Attach Files with Your E-mail

Many e-mail systems let you attach text files and binary files to your e-mail messages. **Binary files** are program files that include formatting and other control characters. Spreadsheet, word processor, graphic, and sound files are examples of binary files. There are many situations in which attaching files is standard practice, such as a collaborative project in which the same program and files are shared among the collaborators. Here are some guidelines for attaching files to e-mail messages.

- Don't send a file when a message will do. Working with files requires extra steps for the recipient, such as decompressing and downloading the file, then starting an application and opening the file. If you're sure the recipient will be able to read the file and it will simplify getting your point across, then send it.

- Make sure the receiver's e-mail system can handle attached files. Not all e-mail systems handle attached files in the same way. It's a good idea to send a test file to make sure both the sending and receiving e-mail systems are compatible.

- Include your e-mail address in an attached document or text file. Attached files are ultimately separated from the original message. Including this information in an attached text file saves the recipient from having to search for the sender's address.

- Be aware that a large file attachment included with your message can cause problems on some e-mail systems, such as the UNIX mail program which is limited to 64K files.

- Use a compression program to reduce the size of a large file you want to attach. Let the recipient know the file is compressed, and check to make sure the recipient has access to the same compression program to decompress the file. Compressing files speeds up e-mail and cuts down on network traffic.

Chapter 3

CHOOSING THE RIGHT WORDS

Choosing the right words for your e-mail messages is the foundation of effective communication. Using the right words makes every word you write perform an important function in a sentence and keeps word fat to a minimum. As a result, your reader's attention is quickly directed to the important points of your message. This chapter explains how to choose, use, and remove words to create clear and concise e-mail messages.

USE VIVID VERBS FOR VIBRANT WRITING

Verbs, words of action, are the principal source of energy in your sentences. Verbs are weak when they're not specific or active or when they depend on adverbs (verb modifiers) for their meaning. Strong, vivid verbs convey direct, vigorous action. Table 3.1 lists some examples of weak verbs and their stronger alternatives. Let the following suggestions guide you in choosing verbs.

- Avoid using weak forms of verbs, such as the present progressive, which is formed with *am*, *is*, and *are*. Compare the following two sentences.

  Flintstones vitamins <u>are</u> <u>lacking</u> the Wilma character.

  Flintstones vitamins <u>lack</u> the Wilma character.

- Don't use *There is, There are,* or *It is* in the beginning of a sentence; they steal the important opening position from more dynamic words.

  There is a Barney marathon starting on Monday.

  The Barney marathon starts on Monday.

- Replace nouns ending in *-tion, -sion, -ance, -ence, -ment,* and *-ing* with verbs.

  The marketing department took into consideration the idea of using Keith Richards as their product spokesperson.

  The marketing department considered the idea of using Keith Richards as their product spokesperson.

Table 3.1 Weak verbs and their stronger alternatives

Weak Phrase	Stronger Alternative
bring to a resolution	resolve
bring to an end	end
do a study of the effects	study the effects
give a promotion	promote
give a response	respond
have a tendency to	tend
have an ability to	can
hold a conference	confer
hold a meeting	meet
make a decision	decide
make changes in	change
make progress toward	progress toward
make a recommendation	recommend
make reductions	reduce
provide a summary of	summarize
take action	act
take into consideration	consider

KEEP TO THE PRESENT TENSE

Tense is the property of a verb that indicates the time when an action takes place. The primary tenses in English are *present*, *past*, and *future*. If you keep to the present tense your sentences will seem more active. The future tense makes a sentence wordy and dilutes its impact. But don't convert the past or future tense into the present tense if the past or future tense is truly needed.

Past tense: *I <u>called</u> the psychic hotline on my break.*

Present tense: *I <u>call</u> the psychic hotline. I <u>am</u> <u>calling</u> the psychic hotline.*

Future tense: *I <u>will</u> <u>call</u> the psychic hotline on my break.*

WATCH YOUR IRREGULAR VERBS

A regular verb forms its past tenses simply by adding the suffix *-ed* to the verb. Irregular verbs form their past tenses by changing their form. They often have different forms for simple past tense and past participle. A past participle is a verb form used with *have, has* or *had.* Table 3.2 lists irregular verbs that can cause problems.

Table 3.2 Troublesome irregular verbs

Present Tense Today I	Past Tense Yesterday I	Past Participle I Have
arise	arose	arisen
become	became	become
begin	began	begun
bend	bent	bent
bring	brought	brought
choose	chose	chosen
do	did	done

Table 3.2 *(continued)*

Present Tense Today I	Past Tense Yesterday I	Past Participle I Have
drink	drank	drunk
drive	drove	driven
fly	flew	flown
forbid	forbade	forbidden
get	got	gotten
go	went	gone
have	had	had
know	knew	known
lay	laid	laid
lend	lent	lent
lie	lay	lain
mistake	mistook	mistaken
prove	proved	proved, proven
ride	rode	ridden
run	ran	run
see	saw	seen
seek	sought	sought
shrink	shrank	shrunk
sink	sank	sunk
slide	slid	slid
speak	spoke	spoken
swear	swore	sworn
take	took	taken
think	thought	thought
wake	waked, woke	waked, woken

CHOOSE CONCRETE WORDS FOR SOLID PROSE

Concrete words paint specific pictures for your reader. Generalities might be convenient to use and come easily to mind, but they force the reader to figure out your exact meaning. Say precisely what you mean by replacing vague words with concrete ones.

Vague: *Please send the information to me ASAP.*

Concrete: *Please send the Cheez Whiz report to me by Tuesday, July 19.*

Concrete words combine both the general and specific; they get the job done fast and efficiently. The following are examples of vague words and their concrete alternatives.

Vague Word	Concrete Alternative
color	red
emotion	hatred
food	steak
scientist	physicist
vehicle	bicycle

USE SIMPLE AND FAMILIAR WORDS

The average person in the United States reads at a fifth-grade level (11 years of age). The average professional reads at about the twelfth-grade level (18 years of age). A word that your recipient doesn't recognize has no power. If a word confuses your readers and sends them scurrying for the dictionary, it has broken their concentration. Simple and familiar words have power. Using them doesn't mean your thinking is simplistic. Potent thoughts are often embodied in simple language.

Complex and unfamiliar: *The bug is agnogenic.*

Simple and familiar: *The cause of the software problem is unknown.*

Here are guidelines for using simple and familiar words.

- Don't use four- or five-syllable words when one- or two-syllable words convey the idea just as well. On the other hand, don't use short words that are so rare your reader might not know them.
- Consider a word familiar if it comes easily to mind but is not part of some specialized knowledge you have. If you never heard of the word until you found it in the thesaurus or if you haven't read it at least a couple of times in the past year, use a more familiar word.

Table 3.3 lists some common simple words you can substitute for complex words.

Table 3.3 A sampler of simple words

Complex Word	Simple Word
abbreviate	shorten
aggregate	total
amorphous	shapeless
ascertain	find out
assist	help
beverage	drink
commencement	start
concept	idea
conceptualize	conceive, think of
conjecture	guess
currently	now
deficit	shortage
demonstrate	show
duplicate	copy
expedite	speed up
facilitate	ease
feasible	possible
finalize	complete
furnish	provide
indicate	tell
maintenance	upkeep

Table 3.3 *(continued)*

Complex Word	Simple Word
obtain	get
optimum	best
parameters	boundaries
prioritize	order
receive	get
terminate	end
utilize	use
viable	workable

WHEN TO USE JARGON

Every industry and profession has its buzz words or lingo, which is referred to as **jargon**. Jargon has two meanings. The first definition is the use of familiar words in unfamiliar ways. The second definition is the use of technical or specialized language unfamiliar to a reader. This second use of jargon causes the most problems. Here are some guidelines to keep in mind when using technical or specialized language in your e-mail messages.

- Use jargon only if you're sure your reader will understand it. Unless your readers are completely familiar with the subject matter, use nontechnical words to describe technical terms.
- Be careful that you don't define a term for a nontechnical reader using additional unfamiliar terminology.
- Don't use jargon to impress your reader; it usually does the opposite.

> **Note:** Gobbledygook is sometimes confused with jargon. Gobbledygook is the use of abstract or pompous words and long, convoluted sentences. It's simply bad writing.

USE CLICHÉS SPARINGLY

The French word *cliché* means "stereotype." Many clichés were originally metaphors that sparkled. This made them memorable, so they were repeated often. However, the vividness of an original metaphor is dulled by repetition; eventually the expression becomes a cliché. Traditionalists frown on the use of clichés, but in e-mail a careful use of modern, reasonable clichés can be an effective way to communicate because they convey concepts quickly. Here are some guidelines for working with clichés.

- Don't use a cliché that clashes with the context in which you're using it. Don't use a cliché that calls attention to itself.
- Use modern, reasonable clichés sparingly. Don't use outdated clichés.
- Keep in mind that your use of clichés should depend on the audience of your message.

Table 3.4 lists some commonly used clichés.

Table 3.4 Commonly used clichés

a can of worms	controlling factor
add insult to injury	dark horse
agree to disagree	days are numbered
at one fell swoop	depths of despair
back to the drawing board	dig in your heels
bite the bullet	drastic action
bottom line	each and every
brute force	eat, drink, and be merry
built-in safeguards	existing condition
burning question	eyeball to eyeball
by leaps and bounds	fall on bad times
calm before the storm	far and wide
chain reaction	far cry
come full circle	few and far between
conservative estimate	final analysis

Table 3.4 *(continued)*

finishing touches	narrow escape
food for thought	nipped in the bud
foregone conclusion	no sooner said than done
give the green light to	one and the same
goes without saying	own worst enemy
good team player	pay the piper
grind to a halt	peer group
heart of the matter	pie in the sky
heated argument	play hardball
hook, line, and sinker	play it by ear
hunker down	powers that be
ignorance is bliss	pros and cons
in close proximity	reigns supreme
inextricably linked	reliable source
in short supply	sadder but wiser
in this day and age	selling like hotcakes
it dawned on me	shift into high gear
just desserts	stick out like a sore thumb
just for openers	sum and substance
keep options open	take the bull by the horns
last but not least	throw a monkey wrench
last-ditch effort	thrust of your report
leaps and bounds	tongue in cheek
lock, stock, and barrel	trials and tribulations
marked contrast	uptight
matter of life and death	vanish into thin air
moment of truth	wear and tear
moot point	word to the wise
more the merrier	

DON'T BE REDUNDANT

Redundant words easily creep into writing. In the rush to write an e-mail message, you might use words that are not only unnecessary but that actually obscure what you are trying to convey. Eliminate any redundant words by paying attention to the subtleties in the meanings of words. Table 3.5 lists some common redundancies to watch out for and appropriate substitutes.

Table 3.5 Redundant words and their substitutions

Redundant Words	Substitution
absolutely essential	essential
absolutely perfect	perfect
accidentally stumbled	stumbled
actual experience	experience
adequate enough	adequate *or* enough
advance planning	planning
any and all	all
as a general rule	as a rule
ask the question	ask
basic essentials	basics *or* essentials
basic fundamentals	fundamentals
check up on	check
close proximity	near
combine into one	combine
completely opposite	opposite
consecutive in a row	consecutive
consensus of opinion	consensus
continue on	continue
contributing factor	factor
current status	status
diametrically opposite	opposite
different varieties	varieties
disregard altogether	disregard
end result	result
estimate about	estimate
exactly identical	identical
filled to capacity	filled
final outcome	outcome

Table 3.5 *(continued)*

Redundant Words	Substitution
first and foremost	first
first priority	priority
foreign imports	imports
group meeting	meeting
honest truth	truth
joined together	joined
joint cooperation	cooperation
main essentials	essentials
mutual cooperation	cooperation
necessary requisite	requisite
new breakthrough	breakthrough
one and the same	the same
overall plan	plan
past experience	experience
personal friend	friend
personal opinion	opinion
plan ahead	plan
point in time	time
postponed until later	postponed
qualified expert	expert
range all the way from	range from
reason is because	reason is
reduce down	reduce
refer back to	refer to
repeat again	repeat
same identical	identical
seems apparent	seems
shuttle back and forth	shuttle
single unit	unit
small in size	small
specific example	example
still remains	remains
summer months	summer
surprising upset	upset
throughout the entire	throughout

Table 3.5 *(continued)*

Redundant Words	Substitution
total of ten	ten
true fact	fact
ultimate end	end
unsolved problem	problem
visit with	visit
whether or not	whether

ELIMINATE DEADWOOD MODIFIERS

Wordiness sometimes is the result of elaborating on things that can go without saying. Modifiers, usually adverbs and adjectives, are often used as a crutch to carry sentences that lack the strength of vivid verbs and concrete nouns.

> **Modifiers:** *For the most part, we all pitched in and ultimately the project was very successful.*

> **No modifiers:** *The project was successful.*

Here are some pointers for controlling modifiers.

- Avoid the most overused modifier of all, *very*. Overusing *very* weakens, rather than strengthens, your message.

- Use modifiers sparingly as transitions from one sentence or paragraph to another.

Table 3.6 lists the most common deadwood modifiers that you should avoid.

Table 3.6 Deadwood modifiers

a bit	as a result	besides
actually	as a rule	by large
also	awfully	measure
anyhow	basically	certainly

Table 3.6 *(continued)*

consequently	kind of	probably
essentially	likewise	quite
extremely	literally	rather
for example	little	really
for the most part	mainly	similarly
	meanwhile	so
furthermore	more or less	somewhat
generally	moreover	still
hence	mostly	then
however	namely	therefore
in addition	nevertheless	thus
in fact	ordinarily	ultimately
indeed	otherwise	usually
inevitably	pretty or pretty much	very
instead		yet

ELIMINATE WORDY PHRASES

Wordy phrases use too many words to express an idea. Most wordy phrases incorporate redundancies. Many e-mail writers use them habitually, so they seem natural. Eliminating wordy phrases from your e-mail messages adds value to every word that remains. Table 3.7 lists common wordy phrases and suggested substitutes.

Table 3.7 Common wordy phrases

Wordy Phrases	Substitution
according to the law	legally
afford an opportunity	permit *or* allow
a great deal of	much
a large number of	many
along the lines of	like
a majority of	most
a period of several weeks	several weeks
as a general rule	usually *or* generally

Table 3.7 *(continued)*

Wordy Phrases	Substitution
as a matter of fact	in fact
as of this date	today
assuming that	if
a sufficient number	enough
as you may or may not know	as you may know
at all times	always
at present	now
at regular intervals of time	regularly
at the conclusion of	after
at this point in time	now
beyond a shadow of a doubt	doubtless
brought to a sudden halt	halted
by the time that	when
called attention to the fact	reminded
can be in a position to	can
come to an end	end
despite the fact that	although
detailed information	details
due to the fact that	because
during the course of	during
estimated roughly at	estimate at
except in a small number of cases	usually
exhibit a tendency to	tend to
for the purpose of	for *or* to
for this reason	so
from time to time	occasionally
if at all possible	if possible
in a number of cases	many *or* some
in a satisfactory manner	satisfactorily
inasmuch as	since
in compliance with your request	at your request

Table 3.7 *(continued)*

Wordy Phrases	Substitution
in light of the fact that	because
in many cases	often
in the proximity of	near
in rare cases	rarely
in the event that	if
in the very near future	soon
in view of the fact that	considering
is in the process of making	is making
is of the opinion that	believes
last of all	last
make a purchase	buy
make a recommendation that	recommend
make contact with	meet *or* contact
more and more	increasingly
notwithstanding the fact that	although
of a confidential nature	confidential
on a few occasions	occasionally
on the basis of	by
on the grounds that	because
on two different occasions	twice
owing to the fact that	since *or* because
perform an analysis of	analyze
pertaining to	about
pursuant to	following
range all the way from	range from
reduced to basic essentials	simplified
repeat again	repeat
revised downward	lower
seldom if ever	rarely
subsequent to	after *or* following
take appropriate measures	act
take this factor into consideration	therefore

Table 3.7 *(continued)*

Wordy Phrases	Substitution
the only difference being that	except that
there is no question that	unquestionably
to summarize the above	in summary
until such time as	until
when and if	if
within the realm of possibility	possibly *or* possible
with reference to	about
with the exception of	except
with the result that	so that

DON'T CONFUSE YOUR WORDS

Mark Twain said, "The difference between the right word and the almost right word is the difference between lightning and the lightning bug." Many words that appear interchangeable frequently are not. Misusing these phrases can often distract your reader and lead to misinterpretations. Table 3.8 lists commonly misused words that are frequently used interchangeably, but in fact have different meanings.

Table 3.8 Commonly confused words

Word	Definition
accept	receive willingly
except	exclude
adverse	unfavorable
averse	unwilling
advice	suggestion or counsel (noun)
advise	give advice (verb)

Table 3.8 *(continued)*

Word	Definition
affect	influence (verb)
effect	to bring about (verb), result (noun)
all	always acceptable
all of	use with a personal pronoun
allusion	indirect reference to something
illusion	a mistaken perception
already	beforehand
all ready	completely ready
among	three or more persons or things are involved
between	a connection involving only two persons or things
amount	use with mass nouns
number	use with countable nouns
anyone	any person
any one	a specific person or object
as	use when you would otherwise use *during*
because	use instead of *the reason being*
since	means *after the time that;* also means *because*
can	has the ability to
may	has permission to
might	is possible to
compare to	represent as similar or equal
compare with	examine for similarities or differences
complement	to complete a whole or satisfy a need
compliment	praise
comprise	contain
compose	create by joining
constitute	make up, form

Table 3.8 *(continued)*

Word	Definition
continual	repeated at frequent intervals
continuous	uninterrupted
desert	arid terrain (noun), abandon (verb)
dessert	sweet end to a meal
desperate	reckless or dangerous because of despair or urgency
disparate	different, dissimilar
disburse	to pay out
disperse	to scatter
discreet	behavior that is prudent or respectful of propriety
discrete	scientific connotation for separate, distinct, or individual
disinterested	conveys objectivity or neutrality
uninterested	lacking interest
dual	composed of two
duel	prearranged combat between two people to settle a quarrel
eminent	well known or distinguished
imminent	about to happen
farther	physical distance only
further	physical or nonphysical distance
fewer	for number
less	for quantity
foreword	short introductory statement in a published work
forward	toward the front
good	an adjective (a good dog)
well	an adverb (a well thought-out design)

Table 3.8 *(continued)*

Word	Definition
imply	suggest
infer	draw a conclusion
insure	make secure, or guarantee life or property against risk
ensure	make sure, certain
assure	set someone's mind at rest
it's	contraction of *it is*
its	possessive pronoun (the dog buried its bone)
lay	to place or put down
lie	to recline, to tell an untruth
loose	unrestrained or not fastened
lose	opposite of *win*
people	for large groups
persons	an exact or small number of individuals
precede	come before
proceed	go on, continue
press	put force on
type	press a key on a keyboard
hit	strike with force
depress	make sad
principal	school administrator (noun); most important (adjective)
principle	rule or standard
stationary	fixed in one spot
stationery	paper for writing on
than	used for comparisons
then	adverb that means *at that time*

Table 3.8 *(continued)*

Word	Definition
their	possessive form of they
they're	contraction of *they are*
there	opposite of *here*
to	preposition
too	adverb meaning excessively or also (conjunctive adverb)
which	introduces a nonessential phrase
that	introduces an essential phrase
which	refers to things
who	refers to persons
who	subjective case; use if *he, she,* or *they* would fit
whom	objective case; use if *him, her,* or *them* would fit
your	possessive form of *you*
you're	contraction of *you are*

WATCH ME, MYSELF, AND I

Most of the errors in the use of *me, myself,* and *I* result from a widespread misconception that using *I* is egocentric and using the word *me* is undignified in business communication. As a result, the word *myself* is used as the all-purpose substitute, and it is frequently incorrect. Here are guidelines for using *myself.*

■ Use *myself* only as a *reflexive* pronoun or as an emphatic device. A **reflexive pronoun** shows that the doer and receiver of an action are the same. It turns the action back on the subject of the sentence.

   Reflexive pronoun: *I made myself laugh.*

   Emphasis: *I would rather do it myself.*

- Don't use *myself* in place of *me* or *I*. To see if you are using *myself* correctly, drop the first person from the sample sentence *Call Bob or myself for a good time.* If you drop *Bob*, the sentence reads *Call myself for a good time.* Replace *myself* with *me* and the sentence reads correctly: *Call Bob or me for a good time.*

Wrong: *Telly Savalas and myself will continue to test dandruff shampoos around the clock.*

Right: *Telly Savalas and I will continue to test dandruff shampoos around the clock.*

Although it is perfectly acceptable to use *I* to refer to yourself in a message, you can go overboard. If you're beginning all or most of your sentences with *I*, besides being redundant, you'll come across as being self-centered. Here are some ways to keep your *I*'s under control.

- Rephrase part of the sentence as a modifying phrase and eliminate the first *I*.

I am the spokesperson for the clinically depressed clown therapy group, and I will be inviting Ronald McDonald to speak at our next meeting.

As the spokesperson for the clinically depressed clown therapy group, I will be inviting Ronald McDonald to speak at our next meeting.

- Refocus a sentence away from yourself and onto the reader by using *you*.

I have compiled a list of delicious spam dishes that I will send you.

You will receive a list of delicious spam dishes from me.

- Make a request instead of a statement.

  I want you to send me a refund for the X-ray glasses.

  Please send me a refund for the X-ray glasses.

AVOID SHIFTS IN PERSON

When you write, you speak from a person's perspective. *Person* identifies who is speaking. It indicates whether the subject or object of the verb is the speaker (*first person*), the person being spoken to (*second person*), or the person, place, or thing being spoken about (*third person*). Shifting the person in your writing is a common mistake that can leave your reader wondering who you're talking about.

Inconsistent person shift: *If porcupine ranchers work hard, you can make a good living.*

Consistent second person: *If you work hard on a porcupine ranch, you can make a good living.*

Chapter 4

TONE, RHYTHM, PERSUASION— AND FLAME CONTROL

Your writing style is a subconscious sum of its mechanics that is larger than its parts. The rhythm of your writing and the attitude you convey play major roles in how the reader responds to your e-mail messages. Readers respond, consciously or unconsciously, to a false tone or awkward writing. This chapter explains ways you can use tone and rhythm to make your messages more friendly and more lively. It also explains tactics and tips for writing persuasive messages and for responding to flaming messages.

CREATE A FRIENDLY TONE

Tone and style are often confused. **Style** refers to the choices you make to create the tone of your message. **Tone** refers to the feeling or impression your message conveys. Think of style as the cause and tone as the effect. The tone of your message can be self-important, joyous, bland, aloof, scientific, or tongue-in-cheek depending on the writing style you use. An inappropriate or fluctuating style repels rather than beguiles the reader. Your aim should be to write in a consistent tone that is appropriate to the message.

Style can be categorized as formal or informal. Many think writing in a formal style in business correspondence projects power. But formal writing can easily convey an impersonal, unempathetic tone that distances you from your reader. The e-mail medium encourages an informal, conversational style of writing because it's an instantaneous and one-on-one medium of communication. Writing in a conversational style doesn't mean that your writing should be an exact duplicate of speech, but it should be personable. Recipients of your e-mail messages would rather deal with a relaxed, friendly, helpful, positive person than with someone who is negative and impersonal. Here are some tips for writing in a conversational style.

- Err on the side of being too informal and conversational rather than too formal. In most cases—with the possible exception of international e-mail—an overly formal e-mail message alienates the reader. Don't adopt a cold, remote, or superior tone in an attempt to sound professional.
- Use words and phrases that come naturally. Guard against the tendency to overwrite.
- Add some humor to make your message a little friendlier. But be careful if you are sending the message internationally—humor doesn't travel well across cultures.

Use Contractions to Make Your Message Friendly

Contractions help writing seem conversational and informal. A contraction lets you achieve a warmer, down-to-earth tone in a sentence. Deciding when to use a contraction or when to use the full phrase is a matter of taste and style. But keep in mind that it's possible to overuse contractions. Here are guidelines for using contractions.

- Use a contraction if you'd use it when speaking the sentence aloud.

- Replace a few of contractions with the written-out phrase if you find your writing contains too many of them.
- Be aware of hidden wordiness in contractions; for example, *I've got a book* should be *I have a book*.
- Avoid using clumsy or seldom-used contractions such as *The boss'll get you for that* or *I should've known.*
- Use written-out words or phrases if you want a more formal tone or if you want to add special emphasis to a phrase.

Avoid Hedging

When you use a word or phrase as a qualifier, you indicate that you are unsure of the accuracy of the statement that follows. This is called **hedging**. Words that hedge are sometimes called **weasel words**—words or phrases that don't present the absolute truth. Hedging engenders loss of confidence and obscures information; it implies that the writer is avoiding responsibility. Sentences are stronger and more authoritative without the word or phrase that hedges.

Hedging: *For all intents and purposes, our company is bankrupt.*

Not hedging: *Our company is bankrupt.*

Table 4.1 lists commonly used words and phrases that hedge. Avoid them unless they are important to your meaning.

Table 4.1 Common words and phrases that hedge

almost	for all intents and
as I recall	purposes
as I understand it	hopefully
could	I imagine

Table 4.1 *(continued)*

I think	might
I would guess that	my best guess is that
if it were mine to do	practically
in my opinion	probably
in some cases	regarded as
is considered to be	to the best of my
it is my observation that	recollection
it is my opinion that	under the circumstances
it is my understanding that	virtually
likely	well, maybe
may or may not be	

Write Positively

If you need to communicate a negative message, try to mitigate it by suggesting motivating actions that will improve the situation. Readers want to know what is, not what is not. Negative words and phrases convey a negative impression, even when you're making a positive statement. Be tactful; avoid criticizing, embarrassing, or offending the reader. Here are some pointers on how to be positive.

- Avoid these common negative words and phrases: *fail, wrong, unless, error, never, not, none, you claim, failed to, neglected to,* or *lack of.*
- Use *when* instead of *if* to express a thought in a positive manner.

   Negative: *If you finish the report, Mr. Sisyphus, I have another one for you to review.*

   Positive: *When you finish the report, Mr. Sisyphus, I have another one for you to review.*

- Present the bad news at the beginning of the sentence or paragraph, followed by the good news.

Although this year's sales are lower than any previous year's, our current profits are higher than last year's.

- Avoid unnecessary use of words with negative prefixes or suffixes, such as *non-*, *un-*, *ex-*, or *-less*.

KEEP THE RHYTHM OF YOUR MESSAGE LIVELY

William Zinsser, in his best-selling guide to writing, *On Writing Well* (HarperCollins Publishers, 1990), states, "Bear in mind, when you are choosing words and stringing them together, how they sound. This may seem absurd: readers read with their eyes. But actually they hear what they are reading—in their inner ear—far more than you realize. Therefore such matters as rhythm and alliteration are vital to every sentence."

The "inner ear" demands some variety. Most sentences have a subject, a verb, and an object; but that doesn't mean sentences need to be the same size, nor that their components need to be in the same order every time. Listen to the rhythm. Does the message have a smooth musical rhythm that keeps the reader's interest? Keep the elements of a sentence dancing so that they create their own rhythm. Another factor affecting rhythm is transition; smooth transitions ensure that the reader doesn't miss a beat in reading from sentence to sentence and paragraph to paragraph.

Create Sentence Rhythm

Sentences play a big role in creating a pleasant rhythm in your e-mail messages. Use a mixture of short, medium, and long sentences. Consider breaking a long sentence into two or more smaller sentences. To test whether your sentence is too long, read it aloud. If you run out of breath, the sentence is probably too long.

Just as varying sentence length can add rhythm to your messages, so can varying sentence constructions. Identical sentence constructions bore readers. Read the following two paragraphs and listen to the difference that result from varying the sentence length and constructions. See Chapter 5 for information on ways to vary sentence length and construction.

> *We had an exceptionally hectic week. We had dinner with the publisher at McDonald's. We haggled and pleaded, then we signed the contract. We feel the project is going to be overwhelming. We will have to work twelve-hour days, six days a week. We probably will still not be able to finish the project on time.*

> *Last week was exceptionally hectic. The publisher took us to dinner at McDonald's. We haggled; we pleaded; we signed the contract. The project is a killer. To finish, we will have to work twelve-hour days, six days a week. Will the project be finished on time? We doubt it.*

Make Smooth Transitions

A transition in writing is a word or group of words that build a bridge from one point to another. The order of ideas affects the flow of your message. Unless transitions are logical and clear, you risk stranding your reader at bridgeless gaps. Think of transitional words and phrases as pathfinders that show the reader the connection between what has been read and what is about to be read. The following suggestions will help you make smooth transitions to transport the reader from point to point.

- Keep your reader on track by repeating key words, using synonyms and pronouns, or adding a transitional word or phrase to connect your ideas.

> *Last week we <u>polled</u> our customers to see if they were satisfied with our new donut-hole delivery service. The*

results of the <u>poll</u> showed that 85 percent appreciated the service. On the basis of this <u>survey</u>, we will be adding three new donut-hole delivery trucks.

- Don't use long-winded transitions. Use transitions that are concise, smooth, and quiet.

  Long-winded: *I have before me your resume and your request to transfer to the donut-hole delivery division. <u>In addition to</u> your resume, I need a list of references. <u>At your earliest convenience</u>, please send me a list of references. <u>In view of the fact that</u> you said you were unsure about changing positions, please let me know if you have changed your mind.*

  Concise: *I received your request for a job transfer to the donut-hole delivery division. <u>However</u>, I also need a list of references. Please send me a list of references, or let me know if you are no longer interested in the position.*

- Vary your choice of transitions to keep your reader's interest.

  Similar Transitions: *I can cook 75 donuts in a minute. <u>In addition</u>, I can drive a donut truck. <u>Additionally</u>, I was the manager of a Dunkin' Donuts shop for the past two years.*

  Varied Transitions: *Not only can I cook 75 donuts in a minute, <u>but</u> I can also drive a donut truck. <u>More importantly</u>, I was the manager of a Dunkin' Donuts shop for the past two years.*

- Don't use a transition if your direction is obvious.

  Table 4.2 lists some common transitions that show the relationship between ideas.

Table 4.2 Types of transitions and their matching words and phrases

Addition

also	and
furthermore	in addition
in fact	moreover
not only	then

Sequence

after	before
finally	first
initially	later
meanwhile	next
now	once
originally	presently
second	then

Comparison

also	and
both	each
in comparison	likewise
together	

Contrast

but	despite
different	even so
even though	however
in contrast	instead
nevertheless	notwithstanding
on the other hand	still
than	though
while	yet

Concession

after all	although
and yet	at the same time

Table 4.2 *(continued)*

certainly	despite the fact
doubtless	even though
granted	no doubt
of course	still though
to be sure	whereas
yet	

Illustration

for example	for instance
in particular	specifically
that is	to illustrate

Result

accordingly	as a result
because	consequently
for	it follows
since	so
then	therefore
thus	

Summary

accordingly	as a result
finally	in conclusion
in summary	on the whole
so	therefore
thus	to sum up

Emphasis

above all	chiefly
equally important	indeed
more important	most important
of course	surely

Table 4.2 *(continued)*

Place

at the front	farther back
in the distance	in the foreground
in the rear	to the center
to the east (north, south, west)	to the left (right)
up front	

Correlation

either . . . or	neither . . . nor
not only . . . but also	

Use Parallelism to Create Rhythm

Parallelism means presenting two or more parts of a thought in the same grammatical form to express ideas of equal importance or for effect. Ideas that parallel one another in content should parallel one another in form. Readers are affected by the rhythm, repetition, equilibrium, and unity of balanced parts. For example, here is a sentence in both nonparallel and parallel form. Note each item in the parallel sentence starts with a word ending in *-ing*.

> **Not parallel:** *The lawsuit against our CEO includes three charges: unregistered vehicle, driving under the influence, and driving while playing an accordion.*

> **Parallel:** *The lawsuit against our CEO includes three charges: driving without vehicle registration, driving under the influence, and driving while playing an accordion.*

The equilibrium and unity of parallelism adds a pleasant rhythm to your e-mail messages. Parallel sentence structure, fully understood and put to use, can bring about startling improvement in your e-mail messages. Chapter 5 explains how to use parallelism in sentence construction.

> **Note:** For a discussion of parallelism in bulleted and numbered lists, see Chapter 2.

HOW TO WRITE A PERSUASIVE MESSAGE

Persuading another person to your point of view is a difficult task. You have to present logical arguments and solid facts to win over your reader. Before you start pounding out your manifesto on a particular subject, evaluate your chances of success. You need to research the facts to back up your position. Stating opinions without supporting facts, statistics, logic, or experience will not convince a skeptical reader.

Facts by themselves rarely convince people to change their opinions. Facts combined with an approach that is sensitive to your readers' needs are much more likely to convince. If you push your ideas too hard, your reader might resist your point of view. Here are some pointers for writing a persuasive message.

- Define the need for whatever you're promoting before you present the facts and features.

- Stress benefits, not features. By emphasizing benefits, you address the reader's primary concern, What's in it for me?

Feature: *The SUX computer <u>contains</u> <u>the</u> <u>Pentium</u> <u>microprocessor</u>.*

Benefit: *The SUX computer, which contains the Pentium microprocessor, runs software five times faster than a computer using the Intel 486-DX chip. This means that <u>you</u> <u>can</u> <u>get</u> <u>more</u> <u>work</u> <u>done</u> <u>in</u> <u>less</u> <u>time</u>.*

- Use facts, statistics, and opinions to support your claims or recommendations, and cite the source or authority that supports your facts.
- Don't exaggerate. If just one fact or figure seems inflated, your reader will likely question your other assertions as well.
- Give an opinion and a logical reason to support your proposition if facts and statistics are not readily available.
- Don't introduce an opinion as fact. If the reader disagrees, you can elicit an attitude of challenge and hostility.
- Replace the phrases *As you know* and *I'm sure you've heard of* with *As you might know* and *Have you heard of . . . ?* Use the phrases *As you know* and *I'm sure you've heard of* only when you're sure that your reader knows what will follow.
- Don't bully your reader into accepting your proposition. Use the phrase *I'm sure you'll agree* only if you're sure your reader really will agree.
- Don't command the reader. Replace the phrase *I need you to* with *Would you please,* and give a logical reason why the reader should comply with your request.

Would you please work overtime on the project schedule this Sunday? I am afraid we are going to lose this contract if we don't turn in the schedule by Monday.

HOW TO RESPOND TO A FLAME

The e-mail medium has inherent characteristics that make it a tinderbox for explosive, emotional e-mail exchanges. Well-worded, tactful responses can douse the flames and win back your reader's goodwill. Chapter 1 discusses etiquette issues that will help you avoid flaming in your e-mail messages. Here are guidelines for taming the flames when replying to a flame.

- Acknowledge the person's need to flame. If the flame is justified, begin by stating that the flamer is right. If the flame is an unjust tirade, you can still thank the person for having brought the matter to your attention. If you are in the right, you can afford to hold your temper. If you're wrong, you can't afford to lose it.

- Take the time to explain thoroughly what led to the problem. People are usually reasonable if you are sincere and honest and come across as being concerned and conscientious.

- Don't get bogged down in unnecessary details or arguments; this will only fan the flames.

- Avoid citing policies that explain why something did or did not happen unless you explain why the policies are necessary.

- Offer the reader reasonable solutions or alternatives in order to rise above the problem.

- If you know the situation has been, or is being, resolved, inform the reader quickly and sincerely. Avoid saying that the problem will not recur unless you're sure it will not.

- Apologize for the trouble, inconvenience, or frustration.

Chapter 5

BUILD BETTER SENTENCES

A sentence expresses a complete thought. Every sentence you write should add value to your e-mail message. Knowing essential sentence-building techniques will help you improve your e-mail message, line by line. This chapter offers guidelines for building better sentences.

USE THE SUBJECT AND VERB FOUNDATION FOR MOST SENTENCES

The subject and a verb are the building blocks of most sentences. The **subject** is the word or words that represent what you're writing about. It is a thing—abstract or concrete—you can name or talk about. A **verb** expresses an action performed by the subject, or it indicates the condition or state of being of the subject. Here are some general guidelines for working with subjects and verbs in sentences.

- Use at least one verb with every subject. A sentence can contain more than one set of subjects and verbs.

- Don't put too many words between the subject and the verb.

  All our <u>customers</u>, from the newest to the oldest, from the richest to the poorest, including our international accounts, <u>must</u> <u>be</u> <u>notified</u>.

  All our <u>customers</u> <u>must</u> <u>be</u> <u>notified</u>.

USE THE ACTIVE VOICE MOST OF THE TIME

The term **voice** in writing refers to the relationship between the actor (subject) and the action (verb) taking place in a sentence. In the **active voice**, the subject performs the action. In the **passive voice,** the subject of a sentence is acted upon. The active voice shows you are taking charge. Sentences written in the active voice are shorter and clearer. The passive voice implies that the author is trying to escape responsibility for what he or she is saying. When you use the passive voice, it might not be clear who or what is doing the acting. Here are pointers on keeping the voice active.

- Supply the subject of a sentence with a verb that makes it do something.

    Passive: *The software license agreement <u>was folded</u> into origami shapes by <u>Bill</u>.*

    Active: *<u>Bill</u> <u>folded</u> the software license agreement into origami shapes.*

- Don't use the passive voice to avoid using the first person pronoun (I, me, we, or us).

    Passive: *<u>It</u> <u>is</u> recommended that the computer system be installed.*

    Active: *<u>We</u> recommend that the computer system be installed.*

- Change the verb to make the sentence active.

    Passive verb: *An increase was seen in the stock's value as a result of the merger.*

    Active verb: *The stock skyrocketed in value as a result of the merger.*

■ Use the passive voice when the actor performing the action is unknown.

The money was found missing while the guard was on duty.

■ Use the passive voice when the object acted upon is more important than the actor.

Technical support—the most important part of our service— is currently being performed in our garage.

MAKE YOUR SUBJECTS AND VERBS AGREE

Errors in agreement are a frequent mistake in sentence construction. **Agreement** means that subjects and verbs agree in number—that a singular subject takes a singular verb and plural subjects take plural verbs. When subjects and verbs don't agree, it can be unclear which word or phrase is the subject of a sentence, especially when a phrase comes between a subject and a verb.

Subject and verb disagree: *Your foot size in our files are correct.*

Subject and verb agree: *Your foot size in our files is correct.*

Here are some pointers to help you keep your subjects and verbs in agreement.

■ Use a plural verb for subjects connected by *and*.

The computer <u>and</u> fax machines <u>are</u> essential business tools.

■ Make sure the subject and verb agree in number. A singular subject takes a singular verb; a plural subject takes a plural verb. The longer and more complex the subject, the more care you must take to make sure the subject and verb are in agreement.

An <u>army</u> of sea monkeys <u>is</u> invading my office aquarium.

- Use a singular verb for singular subjects connected by *either . . . or, neither . . . nor,* and *not only . . . but.*

  Not only the cost but also the design is the problem.

- Use a singular verb if the modifier of a subject or the subject is *each, every, either, neither, one, another, much, anybody, anyone, everybody, everyone, somebody, someone, nobody, none* or *no one.*

  No one was responsible for the drop in sales.

- Make the verb agree with the subject closest to it when one subject is singular and one is plural.

  Neither the programmers nor the designer understands the material.

- Use either a singular or a plural verb with the words *all, any, more, most, none, some, one-half of, two-thirds of, a part of,* and *a percentage of,* depending on the noun they refer to.

  Singular: *All of the e-mail is backed up.*

  Plural: *All of the messages have been deleted.*

- Use either a singular or plural verb with a collective noun (group, committee, team) or expressions of time, money, and quantities, depending on whether the emphasis is on the group as an entity or on individuals or units within the group.

  Singular: *The committee is holding a meeting tomorrow morning.*

  Plural: *The committee have met, and they postponed the decision until Monday.*

- Use a plural verb if the modifier of a subject or the subject is *both, few, several, many,* or *others.*

Both proposals were unsatisfactory.

KNOW THE FOUR SENTENCE TYPES

A sentence is one of four types: declarative, interrogative, exclamatory, and imperative. Understanding and using the different types of sentences in your writing will help you keep your message lively. The following section describes the structure of each of these sentence types and discusses when to use it.

- Use **declarative sentences** to make statements of fact and opinion. When such sentences follow the subject–verb word order, they usually end with a period.

  We reviewed the software specifications.

- Use **interrogative sentences** to ask questions. Interrogative sentences usually begin with a question word (*who, which, where, when, why,* or *how*) or a verb and end with a question mark.

  Have you completed all the necessary testing?

- Use **exclamatory sentences** to make strong assertions or surprising observations. Exclamatory sentences often end with an exclamation point, but keep in mind that exclamation points should be used sparingly.

  What a field day it was for the competition!

- Use **imperative sentences** to give directions or commands. Imperative sentences usually begin with a verb and often end with a period.

  Don't submit the proposal until after the 15th of this month.

USE VARIETY IN YOUR SENTENCE STRUCTURES

Sentences have four grammatical structures: *simple, compound, complex,* and *compound–complex.* These four basic structures can form an infinite number of unique sentences. Using a variety of sentence structures in your writing breaks the monotony of sentences written in the same structure. The following paragraphs explain the four sentence structures.

Simple sentences are sentences that express one complete thought. They contain at least one subject and one verb. You cannot break the sentence at any point and come up with two other simple sentences.

The system is down.

Compound sentences are essentially unions of two or more simple sentences. These simple sentences are usually linked by one of the simple coordinating conjunctions, *and, but, or, for,* and *yet.* A quick test for a compound sentence is to see if you can divide the sentence into two or more simple sentences. Sometimes three or more simple sentences can combine into a compound sentence.

The system is down, and it will not be fixed until tomorrow.

Complex sentences are simple sentences that contain dependent clauses. **Dependent clauses** cannot stand alone but contain some form of subject and verb. *Although the system was down* and *because the system was down* are examples of dependent clauses. Adding a simple sentence to each of these dependent clauses forms a complex sentence.

Although the system was down, we had to work late.

Getting in touch with Hans the technician was our first objective, because the system was down.

Compound–complex sentences are a combination of compound and complex sentences. A compound–complex sentence has two attached independent clauses and at least one dependent clause. An **independent clause** expresses a complete thought and can stand alone as a sentence.

In spite of the system being down, we still increased production totals for the month, but we were not able to reach our goal to fill an additional hundred orders.

Using variety in sentence structure in your writing will keep it from sounding monotonous. Simple sentences should predominate, but don't avoid compound, complex, and compound–complex sentences. If you use only simple sentences, your e-mail message will sound like a see-Spot-run book. Use compound and complex sentences to express related, connected, contrasted, and sequential thoughts.

MANAGE SENTENCE LENGTH FOR READABILITY

Sentence length is an important factor in readability. Readers have to read, comprehend, remember, and interpret information sentence by sentence. The longer a sentence, the more difficult it is for the reader to comprehend the thought being expressed. Long sentences place an unnecessary burden on readers. For best comprehension, the average sentence length should be about twenty words. Of course, *average* means some sentences will be longer and some sentences will be shorter. Here are guidelines for managing the length of your sentences.

- Vary your sentence lengths. Uniform sentence length will make your writing tedious. Make some sentences long and some short.

- Use short sentences for stating clear, crisp thoughts. Short sentences are naturally emphatic; long sentences are not.

- Use long sentences for presenting involved concepts and for elaborating on a point that requires some thought.

AVOID SENTENCE FRAGMENTS AND RUN-ON SENTENCES

A **sentence fragment** is a group of words that does not express a complete thought but is used as a sentence. When two clauses are written as a single sentence without any conjunction or punctuation between them, the result is referred to as a **run-on sentence**. Run-on sentences slow down the reader and interfere with the concise expression of your ideas. Here are some guidelines for avoiding run-on sentences and sentence fragments.

- Fix a run-on sentence by splitting it into two sentences.

  Run-on sentence: *Never trust a rhesus monkey with your wallet it will steal you blind.*

  Never trust a rhesus monkey with your wallet. It will steal you blind.

- Correct a run-on sentence by adding a semicolon between clauses.

  Never trust a rhesus monkey with your wallet; it will steal you blind.

- Use sentence fragments sparingly as a dramatic, attention-getting device. A fragment carefully placed adds force to the previous sentence.

  Rhesus monkeys are thieves. All of them.

CONTROL YOUR DANGLING AND MISPLACED MODIFIERS

A **modifier** is a word or group of words that describes or limits other words. A **dangling modifier** doesn't relate logically to anything in the sentence or is placed too far away from the words it modifies. Whenever you open a sentence with an action using the *-ing* or *-ed* verb form and do not follow it with the name of the person doing the action, you create a dangling modifier.

> **Dangling modifier:** *After discussing PC pricing trends, the decision was made to purchase more PCs.*

> **Correct modifier:** *After discussing PC pricing trends, we decided to buy more PCs.*

Misplaced modifiers are not logically placed in relation to the words they modify. They can distort the intended point of a sentence and leave the reader guessing what you meant to say. The following two sentences send different messages because of the modifier placement.

> *The fire nearly destroyed the entire house.*

> *The fire destroyed nearly the entire house.*

Here are guidelines for preventing dangling and misplaced modifiers.

- Don't place the modifier too far from the word it is supposed to modify.

> **Misplaced modifier:** <u>*Flames licking and sparking,*</u> *the service technician read the user manual while my system burned.*

> **Correctly Placed Modifier:** *The service technician read the manual while my system, flames licking and sparking, burned.*

■ When a modifier dangles, the sentence does not contain the subject being modified. Ask yourself who performs the action implied in the modifier. The answer to your question should be the subject of the sentence. Or you can recast the sentence as in the second example.

Dangling modifier: *While reviewing the program, two errors that should have been eliminated occurred.*

Dangling modifier avoided: *While I was reviewing the program, two errors that should have been eliminated occurred.*

USE PARALLELISM IN SENTENCE CONSTRUCTIONS

Ideas that parallel one another in content should parallel one another in form. **Parallelism** in sentences means presenting two, three, or more items in a sentence in the same grammatical form to express ideas of equal importance or for effect. Parallelism applies to all parts of speech (nouns, verbs, adjectives, and so on), and its consistent use allows you to state your ideas rapidly, clearly, and economically. Here are some pointers for keeping your sentences parallel.

■ Use parallel structures with comparative expressions such as *both . . . and, either . . . or, not only . . . but also,* and *neither . . . nor.*

Not only was I sleepwalking at work, but I was also having nightmares.

■ Use an article or preposition when you are listing items in a series either with the first item only or with each item; it should not be applied inconsistently.

Each item: *The company consists of the manufacturing, the accounting, the advertising, the sales, and the MIS departments.*

First only: *The company consists of the manufacturing, accounting, advertising, sales, and MIS departments.*

- Present series of items in parallel form using either all nouns or all verbs. If you use a verb, be sure to use the same verb form for each first word in a parallel listing. For example, if one item is a **gerund** (verbs ending in *-ing* that act as a noun), make them all gerunds.

Not parallel: *Our investigation will include following the defendant, taking pictures of the defendant in action, and an assessment of the defendant's character.*

Parallel: *Our investigation will include following the defendant, taking pictures of the defendant, and assessing the defendant's character.*

Note: Chapter 2 explains how to create parallel bulleted and numbered lists.

SHOULD YOU END A SENTENCE WITH A PREPOSITION?

Prepositions are words that connect or relate nouns and pronouns to preceding words and phrases. Although there are fewer than a hundred prepositions in English, most sentences contain at least one. The simple prepositions are *at, by, in, on, down, from, off, out, through, to, up, for, of,* and *with.* There are more complex prepositions, such as *against, beneath, in front of, on top of, according to,* and *by means of.*

Under traditional rules of formal writing, sentences should not end with prepositions. When Winston Churchill was chastised for ending a sentence with a preposition, he wittily responded "This is the type of arrant pedantry up with which I will not put." Churchill's retort illustrates that attempts to avoid ending a sentence with a preposition can be labored and ludicrous. Many sentences are easier to read when they end with a preposition. For example, *What are you looking for?* is more natural sounding than *For what are you looking?* Don't incorrectly identify as prepositions those adverbs, adverbial parts, or phrasal verbs *(to set up, to turn on)* that appear at the ends of sentences. These adverbs work well at the end of sentences as long as the whole verb is kept together.

Be sure your printer is turned on.

SHOULD YOU START A SENTENCE WITH A COORDINATING CONJUNCTION?

Conjunctions connect words, phrases, or clauses and at the same time indicate the relationship between them. One type of conjunction is the simple coordinating conjunction (*and, but, or, for, nor, so, yet*). It's an unfair but accepted practice for grade-school teachers to threaten to lower students' grades if they begin a sentence with a conjunction. The purpose of this tyranny is to teach that the primary use of conjunctions is to connect, not to introduce. But we're not in grade school anymore, so you won't be penalized for starting some sentences with a conjunction. Here are some guidelines for using conjunctions to start sentences.

- Express a complete thought when you start a sentence with a conjunction.
- Don't overuse conjunctions to start sentences. As with any device to enhance readability, overuse dilutes its impact.
- Use the conjunction *but* as a forceful way to start a sentence that contradicts or qualifies the information

in the previous sentence. Keep in mind that if you start a sentence with the word *but*, you need to express a complete thought in direct opposition to the previous sentence.

- Begin a sentence with *and* only when you want to make a transition from the previous sentence.

Chapter 6

MIND YOUR MECHANICS

Mechanics is a catch-all term that encompasses several important writing elements, including spelling, abbreviation, capitalization, and numbering. By far, the most important element of mechanics is keeping your spelling in check. Misspellings are abundant in e-mail. This chapter explains how to improve your spelling to keep your messages from having the negative effect of distracting your reader. It also shows you how to use abbreviation, capitalization, and numbering effectively in your e-mail messages.

CHECK YOUR SPELLING

For every grammar mistake in an e-mail message there are an average of three spelling mistakes. If you think that you're saving time by not correcting spelling errors, think again. The time saved not checking your spelling is multiplied by the time that it takes for a reader to decipher the misspelled words. Misspelled words jar your reader's concentration by diverting attention away from the idea you are expressing. Not only are misspellings annoying and confusing, they also cause the reader to question your credibility. Misspellings make you look sloppy or, worse yet, incompetent.

Because the English language has been influenced by diverse sources, its spellings are inconsistent. Good spelling is primarily a matter of forming the right mental associations and developing an eye for words that don't look right. Because misspellings are so frequent in e-mail messages, we list here the most common spelling rules and guidelines for checking your spelling. If you're in a hurry, bypass the rules and go right to Table 6.1 to look up the spelling of troublesome words.

- Don't stop writing your message to look up a word. Check your spelling after you have written your message. Checking questionable words as you write can break your concentration; you might end up forgetting or omitting an idea you wanted to express.

- Use a spell-checker program if your e-mail system supports one. Keep in mind that a spelling checker cannot check for misused words. If you type *wood* when you mean *would*, a spelling checker will not catch it, because *wood* is an actual word.

- Remember *i* before *e*, except after *c*, which works most of the time. The most common exceptions to this rule are *counterfeit, foreign, freight, height, neighbor, science, sleigh, weigh,* and *weight.*

- Keep the final *e* when adding a suffix to a word that ends in *e* if the first letter of the suffix is a consonant. *Achieve* plus *-ment* becomes *achievement, nine* plus *-ty* becomes *ninety.* Drop the *e* if the first letter of the suffix is a vowel. *Achieve* plus *-able* becomes *achievable, rule* plus *-er* becomes *ruler.* Exceptions are words in which the final *e* is preceded by *c, e, g,* or *o* (the final *e* stays). *Agree* plus *-ing* becomes *agreeing, manage* plus *-able* becomes *manageable.*

- Double the final consonant of a two-syllable word when the accent falls on the final syllable and the suffix begins with a vowel. *Admit* plus *-ance* becomes *admittance, control* plus *-ing* becomes *controlling.* In words in which the accent falls on the first syllable, the consonant isn't doubled. *Credit* plus *-or* becomes *creditor, order* plus *-ing* becomes *ordering.*

- Add *-es* to words ending in *ch*, *x*, or *s* to form their plurals. *Boss* becomes *bosses*, *catch* becomes *catches*, *church* becomes *churches*, *tax* becomes *taxes*.
- Form plurals of noun phrases by adding the plural ending, typically *-s* or *-es*, to the word that is modified by its neighbor. Note in the following examples that the modifiers untypically follow the noun being made plural. *Notaries public, attorneys at law, mothers-in-law,* and *by-products.*
- Add *s* to make acronyms, numbers, and letters plural; for example *VIPs, the late '80s.* Lower-case letters or abbreviations with periods require an apostrophe before the plural *s*; for example, *Ph.D.'s, x's and y's.*
- Form plurals for words of Greek and Latin origin that end in *-um* or *-on* by dropping the *-um* or *-on* and adding an *-a*. *Addendum* becomes *addenda* and *criterion* becomes *criteria*.
- Change the final *y* to *i* before adding a suffix to a word, but keep the *y* before words ending in *-ing*. *Activity* becomes *activities*, *category* becomes *categories*, *company* becomes *companies*, *happy* becomes *happiness*, *likely* becomes *likelihood*, *study* becomes *studies*, or *studying*.
- Add the letter *s* to form the plurals of words ending in *y* preceded by a vowel. *Attorney* becomes *attorneys*.

Table 6.1 Frequently misspelled words

A	accuracy	addendum
absence	accustomed	admittance
acceptable	achievable	advantage
accessible	achievement	aficionado
accidentally	acquiesce	aggravate
accommodate	acquaintance	agreeing
accompanied	acquire	aisle
accumulate	addenda	amateur

Table 6.1 *(continued)*

analogous	bureaucracy	controlling
analysis	business	correspondence
anomaly	**C**	courageous
anonymous	calendar	courteous
answer	caliber	courtesy
apology	campaign	credible
apparatus	cannot	creditor
apparent	captain	criteria
appearance	carriage	criterion
appetite	category	criticism
appreciable	cerebral	criticize
appropriate	certain	curiosity
architect	challenge	curious
argument	changeable	curriculum
aspirin	characteristic	**D**
assassinate	charisma	decadence
asterisk	chauvinist	deceive
attendance	coincidence	decision
authentic	commitment	definitely
autumn	committee	dependable
auxiliary	comparable	depreciate
B	compatible	descend
balance	competent	description
bargain	competition	desert
believe	concede	desirable
beneficial	conceited	desperate
benign	conceive	despicable
berserk	condemn	dessert
biased	confident	deterrent
bidder	connoisseur	dichotomy
blatant	conscience	dilemma
bologna	conscious	disappoint
brief	consensus	disapprove
bulletin	consistent	disastrous

Table 6.1 (*continued*)

disburse

discernible

discipline

discreet

discrete

discipline

disease

dispensable

disperse

dissatisfied

dissimilar

dissipate

distinct

doctor

E

easily

eccentric

echelon

ecstasy

efficient

eighth

elaborately

elicit

eligible

embarrass

eminent

employee

endeavor

entirely

entrepreneur

environment

epitome

equipment

equipped

equivocal

errata

erratum

erroneous

esoteric

especially

esthetic

euphemism

evidently

exaggerate

excellent

except

existence

existential

exonerate

exorbitant

experiment

explanation

exponential

F

facsimile

familiar

fascinate

favorite

faze

February

finally

financially

financier

finesse

flammable

flexible

fluorescent

foreign

foresee

foretell

foreword

forfeit

forty

freight

fulfill

G

gauge

generally

geriatrics

gestalt

government

governor

grammar

grateful

grievance

grieve

guarantee

guerrilla

H

happened

harass

heard

height

heir

hemorrhage

heroes

hiatus

hierarchy

hindrance

homogeneous

hoping

Table 6.1 *(continued)*

media	ninety	ordinarily
mediocre	ninth	originally
medium	nonnegotiable	outrageous
memento	noticeable	overreach
memoranda	nowadays	overrun
memorandum	noxious	
microfiche	nuance	**P**
mileage	nuclear	pamphlet
milieu	nuisance	panacea
miniature	numerous	panicking
minor		parallel
minuscule	**O**	paralleled
mirror	occasion	parameter
miscellaneous	occasionally	paraphernalia
mischievous	occurrence	parochial
misshapen	occurred	parole
missile	occurring	particle
misspell	odyssey	particularly
mnemonic	offense	pastime
morale	official	peaceable
mortgage	ombudsman	peculiar
muscle	omission	penetrate
mysterious	omitted	perceive
	omitting	per diem
N	omniscient	perennial
naive	oneself	performance
naturally	opiate	perhaps
necessarily	opponent	peripheral
necessary	opportunity	permanent
neighbor	opposite	permissible
neophyte	oppression	perquisite
nevertheless	optimism	perseverance
nickel	optimistic	personal
niece	orchestra	personnel
nineteen	ordinance	perspective

Table 6.1 *(continued)*

persuade	probably	**R**
pertain	procedure	rapport
pertinent	proceed	rarefy
pharmaceutical	processes	rarity
phenomena	professor	rebel
phenomenon	programmed	recede
physical	programmer	receipt
physician	programming	receive
picnicking	prominent	receptacle
pigeon	pronounce	recession
poison	pronunciation	recipe
politician	propaganda	reciprocal
pollute	prophecy	recommend
possession	prophesy	reconnaissance
possibly	prospective	reconnoiter
posthumous	protocol	recurrence
potpourri	pseudonym	recyclable
practical	psychology	referral
practically	publicly	referring
precede	pursue	regular
precedence	pursuing	regulate
precious	pursuit	rehearsal
preferred		reinforce
prejudice	**Q**	relevant
prerogative	quandary	reliable
prerequisite	quarreled	relief
prevail	quarreling	relieve
prevalent	quarrelsome	religious
preventive	quasi	remembrance
principal	questionnaire	reminisce
principle	queue	reminiscence
prisoner	quiet	renaissance
privilege	quite	renege
probable	quizzes	repellent

Table 6.1 *(continued)*

repetition	siege	succinct
rescind	sieve	suicide
resemblance	signaled	superintendent
reservoir	signaling	supersede
resistance	significant	suppress
restaurant	silhouette	surely
rhetoric	similar	surreptitious
rhythm	simultaneous	surround
ridiculous	sincerely	surveillance
S	siphon	susceptible
saboteur	sizable	suspicious
sacrifice	souvenir	syllable
sacrilegious	spacious	synonymous
safety	sponsor	synopsis
salvage	stationary	**T**
satellite	stationery	technical
savvy	statistics	technique
scarcity	stepped	temperamental
scenario	stopped	temperature
scenery	straight	temporary
schedule	strategy	theater
science	strength	themselves
scissors	strenuous	therefore
secede	stretch	thorough
secretary	studies	though
seize	studying	threshold
seizure	stupefy	through
sensible	subpoena	tobacco
separate	subpoenaed	trafficked
sergeant	subterranean	tragedy
sheriff	subtlety	transferable
shining	suburban	transferred
shrubbery	succeed	traveled
sidestepping	succession	traveling

Table 6.1 *(continued)*

tremendous	usually	warring
twelfth		weather
typical	**V**	Wednesday
tyranny	vacuum	weird
U	vacillate	where
ubiquitous	vanilla	wherever
ultimatum	various	whether
ultimatums	vehicle	whichever
umbrella	vengeance	whiskey
unanimous	verbatim	wholesome
unconscious	versatile	wholly
undoubtedly	vice versa	wield
unmanageable	villain	writing
unnatural	violence	written
unnecessary	visible	**Y**
unnerve	vitamins	yield
unprecedented	**W**	youthful
unwieldy	waiver	**Z**
usage	warrant	zealot

ABBREVIATE TO SAVE TIME

Abbreviations, if used correctly, save time, especially in the fast-paced world of e-mail. Beyond traditional abbreviations, an established collection of widely recognized abbreviations for common phrases has been established in e-mail communications. Here are some guidelines for standard English abbreviations.

- Omit periods for most abbreviations, especially for acronyms, for example, *AFL-CIO*, *AMA*, and *TWA*. Omitting periods in abbreviations is becoming more acceptable in writing.

- Keep the period in abbreviations for shortened words, such as *dept.* or *mgmt.*, or if the omission would create an abbreviation that looks like another word, for example, *a.m.* not *am*. Some abbreviations still require periods, such as country names, time references, titles, and Latin abbreviations, for example, *Dr.*, *e.g.*, *etc.*, *i.e.*, *Mr.*, *Ms.*, *U.K.*, and *U.S.A.*

- Don't abbreviate a unit of measurement unless it is used in conjunction with a number. *The measurements should be submitted in square feet. The office is 25 ft by 18 ft.*
- Use an apostrophe to form the plural of an abbreviation that has periods. *Seventy-three M.D.'s attended the meeting.*
- Abbreviate titles only when you use the person's full name. *Gen. George S. Patton, Gov. John D. Rockefeller,* but *General Patton, Governor Rockefeller.*
- Don't leave out articles, such as *a, an,* and *the,* for brevity. Leaving them out mangles the meaning of your message.
- Don't start a sentence with an abbreviation.

There are a number of e-mail acronyms for common phrases. Originally this e-mail shorthand was used to spare typists from having to key in lots of characters and to spare the computer system from having to use up its expensive disk space. Now they are used as a convenience. Most e-mail acronyms are easy to figure out. For example, a common e-mail shorthand term is *BTW,* which stands for *by the way.*

- Always capitalize electronic shorthand expressions.
- Don't place periods between letters in an abbreviation.
- Don't use e-mail shorthand if you think the recipient of your e-mail message isn't familiar with it.

Table 6.2 lists common business abbreviations.

Table 6.2 Common abbreviations

Term	Abbreviation
also known as	a.k.a.
ante meridiem (before noon)	a.m.
approximately	approx.
et alia (and others)	et al.
et cetera (and so forth)	etc.
as soon as possible	ASAP
blind carbon copy	Bcc
building	bldg.
calendar year	CY
carbon copy to	Cc
cash on delivery	c.o.d.
cost of living adjustment	COLA
company	co.
corporation	corp.
department	dept.
doing business as	dba
each	ea.
end of month	e.o.m.
fiscal year	FY
exempli gratia (for example)	e.g.
for your information	FYI
government	govt.
incorporated	inc.
IOU	I owe you
limited	ltd.
manufacturing	mfg.
merchandise	mdse.
month	mo.
videlicet (namely)	viz.
numero (number)	no.
post meridiem (past noon)	p.m.
postscript	PS

Table 6.2 (*continued*)

Term	Abbreviation
quarter	qtr.
very important person	VIP

Table 6.3 provides a list of the most common acronyms. Here are pointers for using electronic shorthand.

Table 6.3 Common e-mail acronyms

Acronym	Expression
BRB	Be right back
BTW	By the way
CUL	See you later
F2F	Face to face
FWIW	For what it's worth
FYA	For your amusement
FYI	For your information
GD&R	Grinning, ducking, and running
GMTA	Great minds think alike
HHOK	Ha ha only kidding
IMHO	In my humble opinion
IOW	In other words
LOL	Laughing out loud
OBTW	Oh, by the way
OIC	Oh, I see
ROFL	Rolling on the floor laughing
SO	Significant other
TIA	Thanks in advance
TNX	Thanks
TTFN	Ta-ta for now
WB	Welcome back
WRT	With respect to
WTG	Way to go

CAPITALIZE CORRECTLY

Starting a word with a capital letter emphasizes the importance of the word relative to words that start with lower-case letters. Arbitrary capitalization of words to make them seem important leads to confusion as well as devaluating words that should be capitalized. Here are key points for capitalizing.

- Capitalize the first letter of all main words of headings and titles of books, articles, and other documents. Don't capitalize the first letter of articles (*a, an,* and *the*), the coordinate conjunctions (*and, but, or, nor, so, yet*), or prepositions (*by, in, for, to, of, at,* and so on), unless they are the first or last word of a heading or title.

  I read a sample sentence in the The Elements of E-mail Style *that mentioned* Wired *magazine.*

- Capitalize personal titles only if they precede a name and are not separated by a comma. *Chairman Bill Gates,* separated by a comma becomes *the chairman, Bill Gates.* Capitalization is optional if the title follows the noun.

- Don't capitalize the words *government, federal,* or *administration,* except when they are part of the title of a specific entity.

  The federal government *isn't doing its job well. The* Federal Bureau of Investigation *is still tracking the whereabouts of a picture of J. Edgar Hoover in a red dress.*

- Capitalize points of the compass and regional terms when they refer to a specific section or when they are part of a precise descriptive title, for example, *Middle East, Southern Hemisphere, North End.* Don't capitalize words that only suggest direction or position, for example, *east coast, central states.*

- Capitalize proper nouns, but not the words they modify.

  I am no longer a member of the Republican party.

- Don't capitalize the seasons or a.m. or p.m. For example, *autumn, winter, spring, summer, 12:00 a.m., 1:30 p.m.*

- Capitalize the first letter of the first word of a quotation when it forms a complete sentence.

  Lord Acton was right when he said, "Power tends to corrupt and absolute power corrupts absolutely."

- Don't use all capital letters in a message because it makes the message hard to read. Using all capital letters in e-mail is called shouting. See Chapter 1 for a discussion of shouting.

COMMUNICATING NUMERICAL INFORMATION

Numerical information can be represented by numbers or words. How you communicate a number depends on the context in which you're using the number and on the number itself. Here are basic guidelines for writing numbers.

- Use numerals for expressing time, money, and measurements.

  I will be by at 1:00 p.m. to pick up the check for $100.00 for the 12-ft sign you made for our company picnic.

- Write out numbers that begin a sentence.

  Ten million e-mail users can't be wrong.

  Three-thirty in the afternoon is the best time for all of us to get together at the local watering hole.

- Use numerals for dates.

  Mark June 18, 1994, and Nov. 28, 1994, on your calendar.

- Write out numbers one to nine and use numerals for numbers 10 or greater.

  The four team members are 35, 63, 47, and 25 years old.

- Write out large, rounded-off numbers or general amounts of money. But use numerals when expressing specific numbers.

  Rounded Numbers: *Over a million PC users spend over a billion dollars a year on pizza.*

  Specific Number: *My computer is plagued by 134 viruses.*

- Use numerals to write percentages, *2 percent, 50 percent.*
- Use numerals for all decimals, even those less than 10, *1.25, 12.7567.*
- Use *to* or *through* for ranges of numbers in text.

  The number of e-mail users ranges from 30 to 50 million.

Chapter 7

PUNCTUATION ADDS EXPRESSION TO YOUR E-MAIL

E-mail messages lack the visual body-language cues
that exist in face-to-face conversations, things such as
facial expressions, voice tone and volume, and stance.
These nonverbal nuances can be conveyed in your
messages by your use of punctuation. Underuse of punctuation in e-mail can impede communications. In addition to
standard English punctuation, unique e-mail symbols
called **smileys** and **emoticons** can be used to communicate emotional cues. In this chapter you will learn how
to avoid common punctuation faux pas and how to punctuate your sentences to match the intent of your message.

USE COMMAS FOR CLEARER PROSE

Commas can be confusing; it's not always clear if a
comma is essential or helpful. A correctly placed comma
clarifies the meaning of a sentence or phrase better than
any other form of punctuation. Commas serve several
purposes: to introduce, to separate, to enclose, or to
show omission. Because the comma serves so many
different purposes, it is widely used and abused. Here are
some guidelines for using commas in e-mail.

■ Use commas to indicate a brief pause or to prevent
  misreading. If the sentence makes perfect sense when
  you read it at breakneck speed, banish the comma.
  Read the sentence out loud. If it needs a pause for

clarity, add a comma. If your ear fails to help you decide whether to add that comma, go minimalist and don't add it.

■ Use a comma to separate a long introductory phrase from the main body of the sentence. The comma is optional after a short introductory phrase.

Although several employees were slightly injured by the helium tank explosion, the company picnic was enjoyed by all who attended.

In 1994, we will install a new e-mail system.

■ Use a comma to separate a long introductory dependent clause from the independent clause that follows. Usually, long **introductory clauses** begin with words such as *after*, *using*, and *while*.

After reviewing your proposal on brain surgery for beginners, we regret to inform you that we cannot use your book idea at this time.

■ Use a comma to separate a dependent clause from the independent clause, whether it appears at the beginning or at the end of a sentence.

Reading and revising the manuscript, I discovered a coffee stain on page 30.

I need a new copy of the manuscript, because the last twenty pages are stuck together.

■ Use a comma to separate transitional words and expressions—such as *additionally*, *for example*, *for instance*, *furthermore*, *however*, *indeed*, *moreover*, *nevertheless*, *on the contrary*, *on the other hand*, and *therefore*—when they introduce sentences or when they link complete thoughts.

<u>Indeed,</u> the pen may be mightier than the sword, but in a duel I'll take the sword.

- Use commas to separate items in a series, including the item before the conjunction, to provide insurance against misreading. The items in a series may be words, phrases, or clauses. The last item is usually preceded by a conjunction such as *and*, *but*, or *or*.

I'm interested in spandex, dogs, and rock 'n' roll.

- Use a comma to separate two or more coordinate adjectives that modify the same noun. To test whether you should add a comma, check if you can logically link the two adjectives with *and*. If so, use the comma. In the example, *a large squirrel-chasing, cat-hating, yellow Labrador retriever,* you can logically say *squirrel-chasing and cat-hating* but not *yellow* and *Labrador*.

- Use commas to separate independent clauses joined by a conjunction. A **conjunction**, such as *and, nor, or, but, neither, yet, for,* and *so* connects clauses. Don't use a comma to separate the short independent clauses separated by a conjunction.

Independent clauses separated by a comma: *The new computer system works well, but the printer is slow.*

Short independent clauses without comma: *Diana danced the hula and Steve played the ukulele.*

- Precede *etc.* with a comma when it ends a series. It is the abbreviation of *et cetera*. The word *et* means "and" and *cetera* means "so forth," so the word *and* should not precede *etc.* If the list ends with *etc.* in the middle of a sentence, it should also be followed by a comma.

The new advertising campaign consisted of jingles based on Captain and Tennille songs, such as "Muskrat Love," "Love Will Keep Us Together," etc., sung by Meatloaf.

- Use commas to set off nonessential modifiers, descriptive phrases, and clauses in a sentence. A **nonessential clause** or phrase isn't essential to the meaning of the sentence, but adds an idea. You can test to see if a phrase or clause is essential by reading the sentence and leaving out the phrase or clause. Many nonessential clauses begin with the words *who* or *which*.

The new health plan, which doesn't cover hangnails, costs three times as much as the previous plan.

BE DIVISIVE WITH SEMICOLONS

The semicolon is exclusively a mark of separation or division. It's stronger than a comma, signifying a greater break or longer pause between sentence elements. Think of a semicolon as period-like. Here are pointers for working with semicolons.

- Use a semicolon to separate two closely related independent clauses. The use of a semicolon is handy when two statements are closely related and you want to make the connection tighter than it would be with a period, yet stronger than it would be with a comma and a coordinating conjunction.

The computer is a powerful tool; it works round the clock until deadline day.

- Use a semicolon to separate series of words that contain commas. Semicolons can be used to separate phrases or items in a list in which the phrases and items themselves contain commas. Without the semicolon, confusion results.

Raymond Burr portrayed Perry Mason and Ironside; Buddy Ebson portrayed Jed Clampett and Barnaby Jones; William Conrad portrayed Frank Cannon, the Fat Man, and narrated "The Bullwinkle Show."

USE COLONS TO INTRODUCE SOMETHING

Colons are the Ed Sullivan of punctuation. Ed Sullivan introduced the acts for his TV program "The Ed Sullivan Show." Colons perform a similar role; they introduce lists, formal quotations, and examples. Here are guidelines for using colons.

- Use a colon to introduce a list of items, especially when the sentence preceding the list contains the word or phrase *as follows, the following, thus,* or *these.*

  The beneficiaries in my father's will are as follows: Cheetah, Flipper, Gentle Ben, Francis the talking mule, Mr. Ed, and Benji.

- Use a colon before a long or formal quotation.

  Bill Gates started his speech by saying: "Our Windows are shatterproof . . ."

- Use a colon after a clause to amplify or explain the clause. The colon shifts the emphasis to the second part of the sentence.

  Police exist for one purpose: to eat donuts

- Use a colon after a formal salutation.

  Dear Mr. Corleone:

ADD A DASHING THOUGHT

The dash is a vigorous mark that sometimes projects an air of surprise or emotional tone. If used sparingly, it adds a sense of movement to your e-mail writing. The traditional dash mark is an em dash (—). An **em dash** is a dash that is generally based on the width of the capital M, which is the widest letter in most fonts. Unfortunately, the em dash is the only standard mark of punctuation not represented on the typical computer keyboard.

In e-mail, the convention is to use two hyphens without spaces for an em dash. Here are some guidelines for using dashes.

- Use the dash to interrupt—or highlight—a thought. Using dashes to separate parenthetical statements adds a more emphatic interruption than using commas.

  `It's hard to drink in cyberspace--there's no place`
  `to set your glass.`

- Use pairs of dashes to set off parenthetical elements that contain internal commas. Using commas to set off a parenthetical statement that itself contains a comma can cause confusion. Use a pair of dashes instead of commas to make the parenthetical statement clearer to the reader.

  `Over a billion Twinkies--a tasty, undervalued`
  `source of Polysorbate 60--are devoured each year.`

- Use em dashes sparingly. The em dash shouldn't be used as a substitute for the comma.

USE SLASH CONSTRUCTIONS

Traditional grammarians frown on slash (sometimes called *solidus* or *virgule*) constructions, such as *and/or*, *either/or*, *he/she*, and *noun/verb*, because they are considered awkward. In e-mail, slash constructions are widely used because they save time. Whether you use slash constructions depends on the norm for your organization or the audience of the message. Don't overuse slash constructions. If you have too many, they can distract your reader from the purpose of your message.

Please send me the text file and/or the finished documentation.

CONNECT WORDS WITH HYPHENS

A hyphen connects the parts of a compound word. It is also used when a compound adjective could otherwise be misread. The pattern in language evolution is first to join two words with a hyphen and then, after they become accepted as a standard compound word, to make a single closed word. The dictionary is the final authority on whether two words are separated, hyphenated, or joined into one word, so make sure you're using a recently revised dictionary. Here are some guidelines for hyphenating words.

- Hyphenate two words compounded to form an adjective if they precede the noun they modify and if their meaning isn't clear without hyphens. A modifier that would be hyphenated before a noun is not hyphenated when it follows a noun and a form of the verb *to be* (*is, was, were,* and so on), called a predicate adjective.

  We work only on state-of-the-art computers.

  The computers we work on are state of the art.

- Hyphenate compound numbers from twenty-one to ninety-nine and compound adjectives with a numerical first part.

  The thirty-three people in our group turned in a fifteen-page proposal.

- Omit the hyphen between an adverb ending in -ly and the adjective it modifies when they form a compound adjective.

  The artificially inflated figures made the accountant's report look good.

- Hyphenate adjectives ending in *ly* only when they're used with adjectives ending in *-ing*. Verbs ending in

-ing that are used as adjectives are called **present participles**. Other verbs that end in -ing are gerunds.

The book uses friendly-sounding prose to convey its hostile message.

- Use a hyphen to avoid triple consonants and some double vowels: *bell-like, semi-industrial.*
- Use a hyphen in a prefix before a proper noun or number.

In the post-Reagan era, disco is making a comeback.

- Use a hyphen in compounds that begin with *all-, self-, cross-, ex-,* or *half.*

The all-inclusive, self-indexing, cross-referencing, word processing software is only half-written.

TAKE POSSESSION WITH APOSTROPHES

The apostrophe is used primarily to indicate the omission of a letter or letters from words (for example, *isn't* for *is not*) and to form the possessive case of nouns and certain pronouns. The most common mistake people make with the apostrophe is using it to form the possessive case of nouns and of certain pronouns. Here are some guidelines for forming the possessive case of nouns and pronouns.

- Use an apostrophe and an *s* to form the possessive of singular nouns and plural nouns that don't end in *s*.

When it starts, Jim's Macintosh emits a sound like a yak mating.

The men's room is out of order.

- Use an apostrophe alone to form the possessive of plural nouns that end in *s*.

The kids' back-up power supply was driven by an overweight hamster on an exercise wheel.

Don't use apostrophes in possessive pronouns. Use *its* not *it's*, *whose* not *who's*, *theirs* not *their's*.

Whose e-mail message is it, anyway?

- End a possessive word that is singular and already ends with the letter *s* with an apostrophe by itself. Although it is not incorrect to follow the apostrophe with another *s*, it is more common to use the apostrophe by itself.

Bill Gates' heroes include Napoleon Bonaparte, Richard Feynman, and Stimpy.

Bill Gates's heroes include Napoleon Bonaparte, Richard Feynman, and Stimpy.

USE PARENTHESES FOR SIDESHOWS

Parentheses keep explanatory material from complicating a sentence. They indicate an aside that is not part of the main thought of a sentence. Don't overuse parentheses. A sentence should contain only one thought. If possible, put explanatory material or an aside in a separate sentence. Information in parentheses often distracts the reader from a sentence's message. Here are some guidelines for using parentheses.

- Don't make a parenthetical statement longer than the sentence that contains it. If you have a long parenthetical statement, work it into the main text or drop it.
- Use parentheses to introduce acronyms or abbreviations.

Follow the maxim Keep it simple, stupid (KISS).

- Place periods and commas outside the parentheses unless the material within parentheses is a complete sentence. A question mark or exclamation point can appear inside the parentheses only if it pertains to the parenthetical expression.

  When we added up the money spent marketing the Wally the Wacky Woodchuck game (did we really spend over $20,000?), we realized we had spent more than it cost to produce the game.

MARK WHAT YOU DIDN'T SAY WITH AN ELLIPSIS

The ellipsis indicates an omission of words or a pause. The ellipsis, which consists of three spaced periods, is used to indicate an omission within a quotation. Here are some pointers for using the ellipsis.

- Use an ellipsis within quoted material to indicate omissions of words, sentences, or paragraphs.

  "The project delays . . . resulted in a net loss of $3,000."

- Begin a quotation with an ellipsis if the omitted material comes at the beginning of a sentence, especially if the material could be mistaken for a complete sentence.

  Original: *"Despite the new flexible hours for Mondays through Thursdays, all full-time employees must put in a full work day on Fridays."*

  Quote: *". . . all full-time employees must put in a full work day on Fridays."*

- If words are omitted after the end of a sentence, put the ellipsis after the period.

  "If you quote, do not correct mistakes in the quotation . . . . Let the reader see the person warts and all."

- Don't use an ellipsis to open or close a quotation if the quotation is clearly only part of the original sentence.

  Rod Serling defined the twilight zone as "the dimension of imagination."

- Use an ellipsis to indicate a thought process or faltering speech.

  I'm not sure . . . can we do that . . . is that legal?

- Don't omit words from a quotation if it changes the meaning of the original.

DON'T OVERUSE EXCLAMATION POINTS

Exclamation points can be used after commands or statements of strong feeling. However, overusing the exclamation point is as tacky as a Las Vegas lounge act. F. Scott Fitzgerald once recommended, "Cut out all those exclamation marks. An exclamation mark is like laughing at your own joke." You can use the more flexible smiley punctuation, explained later in this chapter, to express a wide range of emotions.

MARK QUOTATIONS WITH QUOTATION MARKS

Words taken directly from another person's speech or writing must be set in quotation marks. To ensure that your e-mail message can be read, don't use curly double (" ") and single (') quotation marks. Curly quotation marks look great, but they don't travel well through different e-mail systems. Instead use the foot (') and inch (") marks on your keyboard. Here are some guidelines for using quotation marks.

- Use single quotation marks for quoted or emphasized words within a quotation.

In China, a Coca-Cola ad used Chinese symbols to sound out "Coca-Cola" phonetically. Coca-Cola withdrew the ad "after learning the symbols for 'Co' 'Ca' 'Co' 'La' meant 'Bite the wax tadpole.' "

- Use quotation marks around a word or phrase you intend to explain or define.

In computer lingo, "biff" means to notify someone of incoming mail.

- Use quotation marks around titles of magazine articles, poems, songs, paintings, and so on. Most e-mail systems don't let you use italic formatting. Chapter 8 includes some suggestions for indicating italics in e-mail messages.

I just read a fascinating article titled "My Life as a Clam," by Shirley McLaine.

- Place a period or comma inside the final quotation mark.

To quote Edgar Allan Poe, "Even where the sense is perfectly clear, a sentence may be deprived of half its force—its spirit—its point by improper punctuation."

- Place a question mark inside the final quotation mark if the quoted material is itself a question. Place a question mark outside the final quotation mark if there is a quoted phrase within a sentence that asks a question.

Ask yourself, "Who am I writing for?"

Did he really say "I'm never sending you e-mail again"?

Note: A common convention similar to using quotation marks is to begin each line of quoted material with the greater-than symbol (>). Many e-mail systems automatically insert the greater-than symbol before each line of quoted text.

PUNCTUATE EMOTIONS WITH SMILEYS

Too often the lack of inflection or facial expression can cause a typed phrase in an e-mail message to be interpreted incorrectly. A visual shorthand using **smileys** or **emoticons** has emerged to help the reader decipher the writer's original intent. Created from keyboard characters, smileys are sideways faces that indicate an emotion. To see the smiley, turn your head counterclockwise. Hundreds of smileys exist. The smiley usually follows after the punctuation mark at the end of a sentence.

I can't wait to see the 2-percent raise in my paycheck. :-|

Smileys are the equivalent of e-mail slang and should not be used in formal business e-mail messages. Also keep in mind that overuse of smileys marks you as a beginner. Table 7.1 lists popular smileys you can use in your messages to indicate a range of emotions.

Table 7.1 Popular smileys

Smiley	Emotion	Smiley	Emotion
:-)	Happy	:-[	Sad sarcasm
:-(	Sad	;-(	Feel like crying
:-&	Tongue-tied	:'-(	Crying
:-<	Really upset	%-)	Happy confused
:-||	Angry	%-(	Sad confused
:-(O)	Yelling	:-*	Kiss
:-D	Laughing	:-\	Undecided
;-)	Winking	:-#	My lips are
:-}	Grinning		sealed
8-)	Wide-eyed	8-O	Shocked
:-|	Apathetic	:-/	Skeptical or
:-o	Shocked or		perplexed
	amazed	:->	Sarcastic smile
:-]	Happy sarcasm	;^)	Smirking smile
	or smirk	X-(	Brain dead

TABLE 7.1 *(continued)*

Smiley	Emotion	Smiley	Emotion
>:-)	Devilish	:-P	Sticking tongue out
O:-)	Angelic		

Expressing emotions in code isn't limited to smileys. Here are some other common shorthand expressions of emotion.

Shorthand	Emotion
<g>	Grin
<s>	Sigh
<l>	Laugh
<i>	Irony
<jk>	Just kidding
<>	No comment

DON'T USE TWO SPACES AFTER PUNCTUATION

Back in your high school typing class, you were told to put two spaces after periods and other punctuation separating sentences. This advice was soundly based on the fact that typewriters use monospaced fonts in which each character takes the same amount of space. Because they are monospaced, you need to type two spaces after punctuation to make a clear separation of one sentence from another. Well, it's the '90s and most computers use proportional fonts, which means each character takes up a proportional amount of space. With proportional type, you no longer need two spaces after periods, colons, exclamation points, question marks, quotation marks, or any other punctuation that separates two sentences.

Chapter 8

FORMATTING AND SPECIAL CHARACTERS ADD PUNCH TO YOUR E-MAIL

In addition to the textual content of your message, there is also a visual element to your e-mail. Formatting tricks and special characters are available on most computers and e-mail systems to make your message more inviting. How far you can go with these enhancements depends on the type of computer and e-mail systems being used by the e-mail message sender and recipient. This chapter explains techniques for formatting and adding special characters to your e-mail messages.

ENHANCE THE PRESENTATION OF YOUR MESSAGES WITH ASCII

A **character set** is the entire collection of letters, numerals, and symbols available on a given system. Most e-mail is confined to the **ASCII character set**, which greatly limits the characters you can use and the ways you can format and emphasize text in an e-mail message. ASCII stands for American Standard Code for Information Interchange, and it's the universal computer code for English letters and characters. All computers can access the ASCII characters numbered 33 through 127, which are the characters on your keyboard. The characters numbered 0 through 32 are control characters and should not be used in text messages. The first 127 ASCII characters are sometimes referred to as seven-bit ASCII. "Seven bit" refers to the number of data bits that are used to specify a character. Characters numbered 128 and up are special characters. PC (DOS and Windows) and Macintosh systems both have special characters available. These special characters—such as copyright and trademark symbols, fractions, and accented characters—are not on your keyboard. UNIX-based systems don't offer special characters as part of their character sets. Working with these special characters is explained later in this chapter.

Even with the limited ASCII character set, you can improve the presentation of your e-mail messages. Different message layout techniques will help you design a document that will attract and hold your reader's attention. The following sections explain how to use standard ASCII characters, available on all keyboards, to enhance and emphasize information.

How to Emphasize Text in an E-mail Message

Because you can't format text in most e-mail messages, a few conventions have been established to emphasize text that normally would be italicized or underlined.

- In e-mail, an asterisk is placed on each side of a word or phrase to indicate that it is italicized. For example, to italicize the word *Fahrvergnügen*, surround it with asterisks.

  The car repair person said my *Fahrvergnügen* needed adjustment.

- To indicate underlining, simply use the underscore character before and after the text you want to be underlined, as shown in the following example.

  My favorite cookbook is _Viva Velveeta_.

Use White Space to Open Up Your Message   The empty space that surrounds text, called white space, makes it stand out. Using an extra line of space between paragraphs or to set apart an important point from surrounding text will make your message more inviting. The following example shows how to use white space to emphasize an important point.

```
Joanne,

Thanks for your message. I will be arriving
at San Francisco Airport on the 28th. I will
be flying on United Airlines. I'm not sure of
the exact arrival time, but I know it's the
red-eye flight.

Could you please pick me up from the airport?

—David
```

Use Tabs to Align Characters   If you try to use the spacebar on your keyboard to align characters at an indent, you'll find that they frequently don't line up. The spacebar method works on a typewriter because every letter takes up the same amount of space, so five spaces always equals five spaces or five letters. This is not always true for type on a computer because many systems use proportionally spaced type. In proportional type, letters occupy different amounts of horizontal space depending on their shape. For example, in a proportional font an *i* occupies a much narrower space than an *M*. To ensure that characters align vertically, use the tab character.

Note: A few computer systems have problems with tabs, but most can handle tabs without trouble.

Use Boxes to Emphasize Important Information You can use the asterisk, hyphen, and pipe characters as graphic elements to illuminate your message. Boxing a key point in asterisks makes it stand out as if it was on a billboard. This is especially valuable when you are mailing a message, an announcement, or other important information.

```
* * * * * * * * * * * * * * * * * * * * * * * * * * * *
*                                                     *
* A boxed message can bring out an important point.*
*                                                     *
*       Use boxes sparingly -- Too many boxes        *
*          make the message difficult to read.       *
*                                                     *
* * * * * * * * * * * * * * * * * * * * * * * * * * * *
```

Here is a sample of text boxed by the hyphen and pipe characters.

```
------------------------------------------------------
|                                                    |
|                                                    |
|     The Meeting Has Been Moved Up One Hour.        |
|                                                    |
|        Meet in Conference Room #1                  |
|                                                    |
|             at 9:00 a.m.                           |
|                                                    |
------------------------------------------------------
```

You can use all caps to make a headline and combine it with a box to grab attention.

```
* * * * * * * * * * * * * * * * * * * * * * * * * * * *
*                                                     *
*            NEW PRODUCT ANNOUNCEMENT                 *
*                                                     *
* * * * * * * * * * * * * * * * * * * * * * * * * * * *
```

> **Note:**   Other ways to enhance important information using more sophisticated graphics called ASCII art are presented later in this chapter.

Include Extra Spaces to Emphasize an Important Point   Extra spaces between characters can also emphasize text. In the following example, each letter is followed by a space and each word by three spaces.

```
P l e a s e     I n c l u d e     Y o u r
C o m p a n y     I D     N u m b e r !
```

Identify Files Included in a Message   The hyphen is frequently used in UNIX-based e-mail systems to identify the beginning of a binary file that has been encoded in ASCII format and included in a mail message. If you're using a UNIX-based e-mail system and have included an encoded file as part of your message, include a line to illustrate where the header and message text ends and the encoded file begins. This way the person can eliminate the header and message text, save the message as a file, and decode the file. For example, a message containing an enclosed file might include the following line:

```
BEGIN-----------------cut here-----------------END
```

Spice Up Your John Hancock with a Signature File
Many e-mail systems let you add a signature file to the end of your e-mail message. A **signature file** is a text file that contains additional information about you. Signature files typically contain your full name, postal address, fax number, other e-mail addresses, and so on. Signature files often include quotes or ASCII logo drawings. However, signatures longer than six or eight lines are generally viewed as wasted space. If you use a signature file, keep it short. How you add a signature depends on your e-mail system. The following is an example of a signature file.

```
--------------------------------------------------
David Angell                 |
dangell@shell.portal.com     |      Bookware
(415) 967-0559 voice         |"Books in about an hour"
(415) 967-8283 fax           |
--------------------------------------------------
```

Have Fun with ASCII Art   Even with the restrictions on artistic expression imposed by the limited ASCII character set, ASCII art flourishes. Creative people have taken the simple ASCII characters and created sophisticated graphic art. These works of art range from slick logos and billboards to cartoon characters like Bill the Cat or Bullwinkle. You shouldn't overload network traffic by loading your e-mail messages with a lot of art, but ASCII art can bring life to a company bulletin or newsletter.

HARNESS SPECIAL CHARACTERS FOR RICHER TEXT

In addition to the standard ASCII character set, there are several other widely used character sets. PC (DOS and Windows) and Macintosh systems both have special characters available. The most commonly used special characters fall into the following categories: quotation marks and apostrophes; fractions; bullets; copyright, registered, and trademark symbols; accented characters for foreign languages; and en dashes, em dashes, and the ellipsis. If you and your e-mail recipient are using the same type of computer and if your e-mail system supports special characters, you can use special characters in your messages. Figure 8.1 shows samples of both practical and fun ASCII art. The following sections explain how to use special characters with PC and Macintosh systems.

> **Caution:**   Remember, you should include special characters only if you are sending a message to someone who is on the same network and is using the same e-mail system and character set as you.

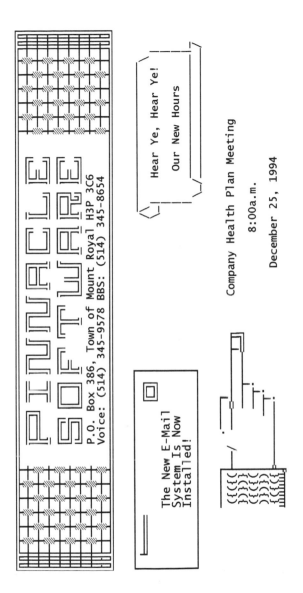

FIGURE 8.1
ASCII art samples

How to Insert Special Characters in DOS

DOS supports the IBM/Microsoft special eight-bit ASCII character set; this set is commonly referred to as the PC-8 character set. Using eight data bits lets you specify 256 unique combinations, which makes available more special characters. The PC-8 character set (shown in Table 8.1) includes extended characters numbered 128 through 255. The special characters with values of 176 through 223 are useful in the creation of graphic images such as boxes. How you include special characters in an e-mail message depends on the text editor or the e-mail system you're using. In most cases, you can include a character that is not on the keyboard by doing the following:

1. Press the Num Lock key to toggle the numeric keypad to on.

2. Hold down the Alt key.

3. Type the numeral equivalent of the ASCII character you want. Be sure to use the numeric keypad.

4. Release the Alt key.

How to Insert Special Characters in Windows

Microsoft Windows supports the **ANSI** (American National Standards Institute) **character set.** The ANSI character set includes the same first 127 characters of the ASCII character set. The additional characters include some foreign-language accented letters and various symbols and typographical marks. Some of the characters from character 127 to 160 can vary from application to application. Table 8.2 shows the standard ANSI character set.

Windows includes a special utility called Character Map that lets you point and click on a character to copy the character to the Clipboard. From there it can be inserted into other applications. Figure 8.2 shows the Character Map window. You can insert ANSI characters

Table 8.1 PC-8 character set

Numeric Code	Character	Numeric Code	Character
128	Ç	160	á
129	ü	161	í
130	é	162	ó
131	â	163	ú
132	ä	164	ñ
133	à	165	Ñ
134	å	166	a
135	ç	167	o
136	ê	168	¿
137	ë	169	⌐
138	è	170	¬
139	ï	171	½
140	î	172	¼
141	ì	173	¡
142	Ä	174	«
143	Å	175	»
144	É	176	░
145	æ	177	▒
146	Æ	178	▓
147	ô	179	│
148	ö	180	┤
149	ò	181	╡
150	û	182	╢
151	ù	183	╖
152	ÿ	184	╕
153	Ö	185	╣
154	Ü	186	║
155	¢	187	╗
156	£	188	╝
157	¥	189	╜
158	P$_t$	190	╛
159	ƒ	191	┐

Table 8.1 (continued)

Numeric Code	Character	Numeric Code	Character
192	└	224	α
193	┴	225	β
194	┬	226	Γ
195	├	227	π
196	─	228	Σ
197	┼	229	σ
198	╞	230	μ
199	╟	231	τ
200	╚	232	Φ
201	╔	233	Θ
202	╩	234	Ω
203	╦	235	δ
204	╠	236	∞
205	=	237	$\emptyset$
206	╬	238	$\in$
207	╧	239	$\cap$
208	╨	240	$\equiv$
209	╤	241	$\pm$
210	╥	242	$\leq$
211	╙	243	$\geq$
212	╘	244	$\lceil$
213	╒	245	$\rfloor$
214	╓	246	$\div$
215	╫	247	$\approx$
216	╪	248	$^\circ$
217	┘	249	$\bullet$
218	┌	250	$\cdot$
219	█	251	$\sqrt{}$
220	▄	252	n
221	▌	253	2
222	▐	254	■
223	▀	255	

into an e-mail message using the Character Map and a Windows e-mail program using the following steps.

1. Double-click the Character Map icon in the Accessories group.

2. Double-click on the character you want to add.

3. Choose the Copy button.

4. Choose the Close button.

5. Choose the Paste command from the Edit menu in your Windows e-mail package.

Most Microsoft Windows applications also let you manually add special characters without using the Character Map by doing the following:

1. Press the Num Lock key to toggle the numeric keypad to on.

2. Hold down the Alt key.

3. Press 0 on the numeric keypad.

4. Enter equivalent of the ANSI character you want.

5. Release the Alt key.

Using the PC-8 Character Set in Windows

The ANSI character set contains many, but not all, of the same characters that are in the PC-8 character set, although the two sets use different numbers for their characters. If you know the number of a character in the PC-8 character set and if the character exists in the ANSI character set, you can use that number to insert the character into your e-mail message. Just toggle Num Lock to on and use the Alt key and PC-8 character number as you would in a DOS application (don't put a zero in front of the number). Windows translates the PC-8 character number into the equivalent ANSI character

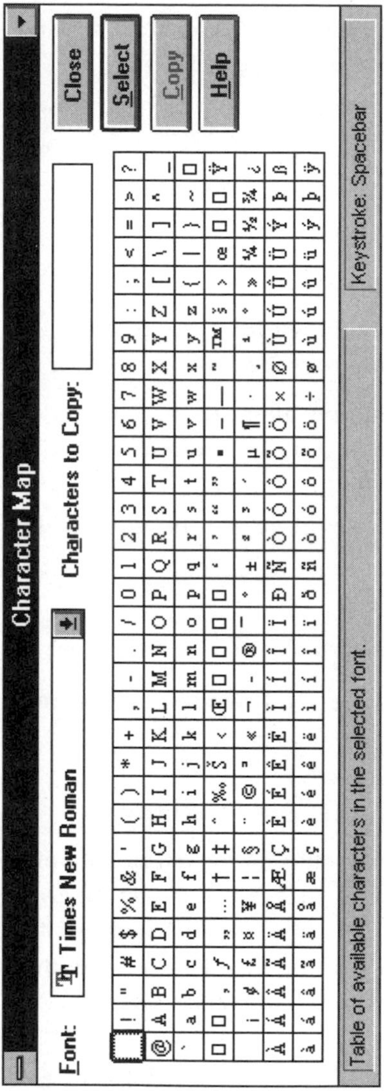

FIGURE 8.2
The Windows
Character Map

TABLE 8.2 ANSI character set

Numeric Code	Character	Numeric Code	Character
130	,	169	©
131	ƒ	170	ª
132	,,	171	«
133	…	172	¬
134	†	173	-
135	‡	174	®
136	^	175	¯
137	‰	176	°
138	Š	177	±
139	‹	178	^{2}
140	Œ	179	^{3}
145	'	180	´
146	'	181	µ
147	"	182	¶
148	"	183	·
149	•	184	،
150	–	185	^{1}
151	—	186	º
152	~	187	»
153	™	188	¼
154	š	189	½
155	›	190	¾
156	œ	191	¿
159	Ÿ	192	À
161	¡	193	Á
162	¢	194	Â
163	£	195	Ã
164	¤	196	Ä
165	¥	197	Å
166	¦	198	Æ
167	§	199	Ç
168	¨	200	È

Table 8.2 *(continued)*

Numeric Code	Character	Numeric Code	Character
201	É	228	ä
202	Ê	229	å
203	Ë	230	æ
204	Ì	231	ç
205	Í	232	è
206	Î	233	é
207	Ï	234	ê
208	Ð	235	ë
209	Ñ	236	ì
210	Ò	237	í
211	Ó	238	î
212	Ô	240	ð
213	Õ	241	ñ
214	Ö	242	ò
215	×	244	ô
216	Ø	245	õ
217	Ù	246	ö
218	Ú	247	÷
219	Û	248	ø
220	Ü	249	ù
221	Ý	250	ú
222	Þ	251	û
223	ß	252	ü
224	à	253	ý
225	á	254	þ
226	â	255	ÿ
227	ã		

number. If the character does not exist in both sets, however, you will get a random character instead of the one you want.

How to Insert Special Characters on the Macintosh

Beyond the first 127 characters, the characters in the Macintosh ASCII character set are different from those in the PC-based character sets. Once you get above character 127, you need to know what you're working with. Characters 127 and 215 through 255 can differ from font to font. Table 8.3 lists characters above 127 using the Macintosh Times font. With the Macintosh, you insert special ASCII characters using the option key in combination with another key.

Table 8.3 Macintosh ASCII Character Set

Numeric Code	Key Combination	Character
128	Option-U, Shift-A	Ä
129	Shift-Option-A	Å
130	Shift-Option-C	Ç
131	Option-E, Shift-E	É
132	Option-N, Shift-N	Ñ
133	Option-U, Shift-O	Ö
134	Option-U, Shift-U	Ü
135	Option-E, A	á
136	Option-~, A	à
137	Option-I, A	â
138	Option-U, A	ä
139	Option-N, A	ã
140	Option-A	å
141	Option-C	ç
142	Option-E, E	é
143	Option-~, E	è
144	Option-I, E	ê
145	Option-U, E	ë
146	Option-E, I	í
147	Option-~, I	ì
148	Option-I, I	î
149	Option-U, I	ï

Table 8.3 *(continued)*

Numeric Code	Key Combination	Character
150	Option-N, N	ñ
151	Option-E, O	ó
152	Option-~, O	ò
153	Option-I, O	ô
154	Option-U, O	ö
155	Option-N, O	õ
156	Option-E, U	ú
157	Option-~, U	ù
158	Option-I, U	û
159	Option-U, U	ü
160	Option-T	†
161	Shift-Option-8	°
162	Option-4	¢
163	Option-3	£
164	Option-6	§
165	Option-8	•
166	Option-7	¶
167	Option-S	ß
168	Option-R	®
169	Option-G	©
170	Option-2	™
171	Option-E, Spacebar	´
172	Option-U, Spacebar	¨
173	Option-=	≠
174	Shift-Option-'	Æ
175	Shift-Option-O	Ø
176	Option-5	∞
177	Shift-Option-=	±
178	Option-,	≤
179	Option-.	≥
180	Option-Y	¥
181	Option-M	µ
182	Option-D	∂
183	Option-W	Σ

Table 8.3 *(continued)*

Numeric Code	Key Combination	Character
184	Shift-Option-P	P
185	Option-P	π
186	Option-B	∫
187	Option-9	ª
188	Option-0	º
189	Option-Z	Ω
190	Option-'	æ
191	Option-O	ø
192	Shift-Option-?	¿
193	Option-1	¡
194	Option-L	¬
195	Option-V	√
196	Option-F	ƒ
197	Option-X	≈
198	Option-D	∂
199	Option-\	«
200	Shift-Option-\	»
201	Option-;	…
202	Option-Spacebar	fixed space
203	Option-~, Shift-A	À
204	Option-N, Shift-A	Ã
205	Option-N, Shift-0	Õ
206	Shift-Option-Q	Œ
207	Option-Q	œ
208	Option-hyphen	–
209	Shift-Option-hyphen	—
210	Option-[	"
211	Shift-Option-[	"
212	Option-]	'
213	Shift-Option-]	'
214	Option-/	÷
215	Shift-Option-V	◊
216	Option-U, Y	ÿ
217	Shift-Option-~	Ÿ
218	Shift-Option-1	⁄

Table 8.3 *(continued)*

Numeric Code	Key Combination	Character
219	Shift-Option-2	¤
220	Shift-Option-3	‹
221	Shift-Option-4	›
222	Shift-Option-5	fi
223	Shift-Option-6	fl
224	Shift-Option-7	‡
225	Shift-Option-9	·
226	Shift-Option-O	‚
227	Shift-Option-W	„
228	Shift-Option-E	‰
229	Option-i, Shift-A	Â
230	Option-E, Shift-E	É
231	Shift-Option-Y	Á
232	Shift-Option-U	Ë
233	Shift-Option-I	È
234	Shift-Option-S	ß
235	Shift-Option-D	Î
236	Shift-Option-F	Ï
237	Shift-Option-G	Ì
238	Shift-Option-H	Ó
239	Shift-Option-J	Ô
240	Shift-Option-K	
241	Shift-Option-L	Ò
242	Shift-Option-;	Ú
243	Shift-Option-Z	Û
244	Shift-Option-X	Ù
245	Shift-Option-B	ı
246	Shift-Option-N	ˆ
247	Shift-Option-M	˜
248	Shift-Option-,	¯
249	Shift-Option-.	˘
250	Option-H	˙
251	Option-K	°

Glossary

ENGLISH AND E-MAIL JARGON

Abbreviations   Form of shorthand used to avoid cumbersome repetition of commonly used phrases. In addition to standard business abbreviations, e-mail has its own unique collection of abbreviations; for example, *BTW* stands for *by the way*.

Active voice   Subject performs the action in a sentence. Active sentences make your writing more lively. They have three basic elements: (1) the actor, which is the person or thing performing the action, (2) the action, which is the verb, and (3) the receiver, which is the person or thing receiving the action. *I wrote an e-mail message.*

Adjective   Modifier that describes or modifies nouns and other adjectives. It can be a single word, a phrase, or a clause. *The clear and concise prose made the message understandable.*

Adverb   Modifier of a verb, an adjective, or another adverb. It can be a word, phrase, or clause. Adverbs give the how, where, when, and extent of action within a sentence. *The presentation was surprisingly successful.*

Agreement   Basic grammatical rule that a subject and verb must agree in number. A singular subject takes a singular verb; a plural subject takes a plural verb.

Alias   Single word or number that stands for one or more e-mail addresses. Aliases simplify addressing e-mail messages.

ANSI character set   Character set used by Microsoft Windows. ANSI stands for American National Standards Institute. Its special characters are different from those in the PC-8 character set. See *ASCII character set.*

Antecedent   Noun or a noun phrase to which a pronoun refers. A basic principle of pronoun usage is that pronouns must agree with their antecedents in person, number, and gender. *She is the person who wrote the message. The new e-mail system has its advantages and disadvantages.*

Article   The words *a, an,* and *the.*

ASCII character set   Universal character set supported by most computer systems. ASCII stands for American Standard Code for Information Interchange. The term is frequently used for both the seven-bit ASCII character set, which includes 128 codes, and the IBM/Microsoft Extended ASCII or PC-8 character set, which includes 256 codes.

Attachment   Text or binary file sent in addition to or as a part of an e-mail message.

Bcc line   Blind carbon copy line. The line in an e-mail message in which you enter e-mail addresses for sending a carbon copy of the message. When you send a blind carbon copy, the recipient of the message named on the To line does not know a copy has been sent.

Binary file   File that includes unique control codes. A binary file is usually a file that can be executed as a program or a file that contains special formatting codes.

Blathering   Posting an article that doesn't get to the point. Blatherers are bad writers who write screenfuls of text that could be reduced to a sentence or two. Blatherers responding to an article will include the entire article in their reply rather than edit it to make a point.

Body   Part of an e-mail message that contains the message text.

Bozo filter   See *kill file.*

Cc line   Carbon copy line. The line in an e-mail message in which you enter e-mail addresses for sending a carbon copy of the message to other people besides the recipient.

Character set   Complete set of characters that are available on a computer system. The character set can include alphabetical, numerical, and symbolic characters.

Clause   Group of related words that contains a subject and verb. There are two main categories of clauses: *dependent* (also called *subordinate*) and *independent*.

Clichés   Common, overused phrases that have become a part of everyday language. *I was up late <u>burning the midnight oil</u>.*

Collective noun   Noun in singular form that refers to a group of persons, places, or things, such as *army*, *committee*, *group*, and *team*.

Common noun   One of two major classes of nouns. Common nouns refer to nonspecific persons, places, things, or activities and begin with a lower-case letter.

Complex sentence   Sentence that consists of an independent clause and a dependent clause. Adding a dependent clause to a simple sentence forms a complex sentence. *I will fix your computer when I'm back from my vacation.*

Compound–complex sentence   Combination of compound and complex sentences: A compound–complex sentence has two attached independent clauses and at least one dependent clause. *Although the computer was not working, I still turned the report in on time; however, I will need to resubmit the report at our next meeting.*

Compound sentence   Two or more simple sentences usually linked by one of the simple coordinating conjunctions *and, but, or, for,* and *yet* or by a semicolon. *The computer was not working, and the technician was not available.*

Compound words   Word formed when two or more words act together. Generally, compound words are written either as one word or as words joined by hyphens; for example, *all-inclusive, deep-rooted, re-create.*

Conjunction   Word or group of words that connects other words or groups of words in sentences. There are two types of conjunctions: *coordinating* and *subordinating.* Coordinating conjunctions—*and, but, or, nor, for, however, moreover, then, therefore, yet, still, both/and, not only/but also, either/or, neither/nor*—connect words, phrases, or clauses of equal rank. Subordinating conjunctions—*as, as if, because, before, if, since, that, till, unless, when, where, whether*—connect clauses of unequal rank (an independent and a dependent clause).

Contraction   Word formed by combining and shortening two words. One or more of the letters is replaced with an apostrophe; for example, *it's* for *it is* and *you're* for *you are.*

Control character   Special character that is not printed but causes a visible result on the printed or displayed output. For example, word spaces, tab spaces, and new lines are all achieved by means of control characters.

Cross-posting   Posting the same article to more than one newsgroup.

Dangling modifier   Modifier with an unclear referent. When you begin a sentence with action that is stated with a verb ending in *-ing* or *-ed* and you do not follow it with the name of the person or thing doing the action, you have a dangling modifier. *Receiving the message, the contract was canceled* is an example of a sentence with a dangling modifier.

Declarative sentence   Statement of fact or opinion. Usually such sentences follow the subject–verb word order and end with a period. *I know the answer.*

Dependent clause   Also known as a *subordinate* clause. A group of related words that includes a subject and predicate but cannot logically stand alone as a complete sentence. *Although we had good weather* is an example of a dependent clause.

em dash   Generally based on the width of the capital M, which is the widest letter in most fonts. Used as punctuation to interrupt or highlight a thought in a sentence.

Essential clause   Also known as a *restrictive clause*. A cause that so limits the meaning of the sentence that without the clause the essential meaning of the sentences would be lost. Essential clauses are frequently introduced by *that* or *who*. *The computer <u>that</u> is <u>in my office</u> is used by several other employees.*

Exclamatory sentence   Makes a strong assertion or surprising observation. Exclamatory sentences often end with an exclamation point. *Help, I erased all my e-mail!*

Executive summary   Short paragraph or section that precedes a lengthy document to highlight its key points. It is designed for people who don't have the time to read the full text, but need to know what the document contains.

Filters   Utility programs that let users sort incoming e-mail into a priority system according to various criteria, such as who the sender is or certain key words in the subject line or message text.

Flame   In e-mail jargon, an inflammatory remark or message. Also used as a verb. Firing angry messages back and forth is known as a *flame war* or *flame fest*.

Future tense   Form of a verb that expresses actions that will take place at some time in the future. *I <u>will</u> <u>send</u> you the file.*

Gender   Term used in connection with nouns and pronouns to distinguish words that relate to males, such as *he* and *man*, or females, such as *she* and *woman*. Nouns that refer to either males or females, such as *person*, are neutral in gender.

Gerund   Form of a verb ending with *-ing* that serves as a noun. We enjoy *writing*. See also *participle*.

Header   First part of an e-mail message; contains address information such as recipient's name and address, subject, and names and addresses to which carbon copies are to be sent.

Heading   Text that is used as a label for material that follows it. Headings are often short phrases and provide logical divisions in long documents.

Hedging   Word or phrase that serves as a qualifier, which indicates that you are unsure of the accuracy of the statement that follows.

Holy war   Flames that have gone on for years. One on-going holy war deals with the question of whether the IBM PC or the Mac is a better computer.

Imperative sentence   Statement that gives a direction or command. Imperative sentences usually begin with a verb and often end with a period. *Send me the file. Stop!*

Inbox   Also known as *mailbox*. The storage area that holds all received e-mail messages addressed to your personal electronic mailbox address. An inbox is a special directory or file for storing e-mail messages.

Indefinite pronoun   Pronoun that has a nonspecific antecedent such as *one, some, anyone,* and *somebody*.

Independent clause   Group of related words that has a subject and predicate and can stand on its own as a complete sentence.

Infinitive   Form of a verb used with the word *to*, such as *to eat, to drink, to recover*.

Interrogative sentence   Asks a question. Interrogative sentences usually begin with a question word (*who, which, where, when, why,* and *how*) or with a verb and end with a question mark. *Who sent the file?*

Jargon   Technical or specialized language unfamiliar to the general reader. Jargon can also refer to the use of familiar words in unfamiliar ways.

Justification   Method of aligning text at the left and right margins.

Kill file   News reader filter program that allows you to screen out postings by a particular user or a particular subject. Also referred to as a *bozo filter*.

Lurker   Anyone who reads but never posts articles on a newsgroup.

Message   In the context of e-mail, an electronic form of communication that typically includes a header for addresses, a body for message text, and optional features for file attachments.

Message text area   Contains the body of an e-mail message. Common text-editing features such as cut, copy, and paste are usually available for writing messages.

Misplaced modifier   Modifier that is not logically placed in relation to the words it modifies. A misplaced modifier can distort the intended point of a sentence and leave the reader guessing what you meant to say.

Modifier   Word or group of words that describes or brings into a more limited perspective other words. Two common categories of modifiers are adverbs and *adjectives*.

Net saints   Experienced Internet users who are willing to share their knowledge with newcomers.

Net weenies   Internet users who enjoy insulting other users by posting flames of any kind, from spelling and grammar criticisms to just plain nasty messages. They fan the flames of holy wars and attack anyone recommending that they take their discussion to e-mail.

Newsgroups   USENET discussions. A newsgroup focuses on a particular topic and contains articles or messages related to that topic that are posted by individuals.

Nonessential clause   Also known as a *nonrestrictive* clause. A relative clause that contributes information in a sentence but is not essential to the meaning of the sentence. Nonessential clauses are usually introduced by *which* or *who* and are set off from the rest of the sentence by commas. *The nonessential clause, <u>which</u> <u>causes</u> <u>the</u> <u>sentence</u> <u>to</u> <u>run</u> <u>off</u> <u>the</u> <u>screen,</u> can be left out.*

Noun   Word that names a person, place, thing, quality, or act. *Common nouns* refer to any person, place, thing, or idea. *Proper nouns* are specific names and begin with a capital letter.

Object   Word or group of words that receives or is affected by the action of a verb. *I bought <u>a</u> <u>Macintosh</u>.*

Parallelism   Convention in sentence construction that similar ideas should be expressed in a similar fashion, thereby demonstrating their similarity and making reading easier. Usually parallelism means using the same grammatical form for a series of items, such as an *-ing* verb form to begin each item in a list.

Participle   Form of a verb that has some of the properties of an adjective and some of a verb. Like an adjective, it can modify a noun or pronoun; like a verb, it has tense and can take an object. For example, *hoping, making, advertising, asked, having lost.*

Passive voice   Opposite of the active voice. When the passive voice is used, the subject is acted upon. Passive sentences are often weaker than active sentences. *Mail was sent to you.*

Past tense   Action or state of being completed at a definite time in the past.

Person   Term used in connection with verbs and pronouns. It indicates whether the subject or object of the verb is the speaker (*first person*), the person being spoken to (*second person*), or the person, place, or thing being spoken about (*third person*). *I liked this guide* (first person). *You liked this guide* (second person). *She liked this guide* (third person).

Personal pronoun   Pronoun that refers to people, such as *I, you, he, she, we, they.*

Phrase   Group of closely related words. Unlike a clause, a phrase does not contain a subject and a predicate.

Plural   More than one. The plural form of most nouns and pronouns is signaled by its spelling. The regular pattern is to add an *-s* or *-es* to the singular form. Irregular plurals don't follow the regular pattern for making a singular noun or pronoun plural. For example, *mouse* and *mice, medium* and *media, I* and *we.*

Possessive   Form of nouns and pronouns that shows ownership (*Bill's strategy*).

Predicate   One of the two major components of a sentence. It includes all the words—and, in particular, the verb—that relate to the subject's state of being or any action taken by the subject. *Barbara <u>has</u> <u>answered</u> <u>all</u> <u>my</u> <u>questions.</u>*

Prefix   Group of letters added to the beginning of a word to create a new word or to alter the word's meaning. For example, the prefix *un-* can be added to *delete* to form *undelete.*

Preposition   Word or group of words that shows the relation between its object and some other word in the sentence. Some common prepositions include *at, by, in, on, down, from, off, out, through, to, up, for, of,* and *with.* The preposition and its object together form a *prepositional phrase.*

Present participle   Verbs ending in *-ing* that are used as adjectives.

Present tense   Form of a verb that covers an action or state of being that is currently going on. It's also used for statements that express general ideas or universal truths. *I think.*

Pronoun   Word that takes the place of a noun. Common pronouns include *I, me, you, he, him, she, her, they, them, who, what, that.*

Proper noun   One of two major classes of nouns. Proper nouns name specific persons, places, or things and begin with a capital letter.

Receipt   Option available on most e-mail systems that lets you ask for a receipt verifying that the recipient of a message has opened it. This is the electronic equivalent of certified mail.

Reflexive pronoun   Shows that the doer and receiver of an action are the same. It turns the action back on the subject of the sentence. *The technician electrocuted himself.*

Reply   E-mail system feature that lets you reply to a message directly from your inbox. The reply feature automatically addresses the e-mail message to the person who sent the original message and inserts the subject line of the original message in the reply message's subject line.

Run-on sentence   Two clauses written as a single sentence without any conjunction or punctuation between them.

Sentence   Group of words that stands on its own as a complete thought. A sentence normally contains a subject and predicate. It begins with a capital letter and ends with a period, a question mark, or an exclamation point.

Sentence fragment   Group of words that does not express a complete thought but is used as a sentence.

Sexist language   Words that indicate a male or female bias.

Shouting   Typing an e-mail message in all uppercase letters.

Signature file   Text file containing information about the sender that is inserted at the bottom of e-mail messages.

Simple sentence   Sentence that expresses one complete thought. A simple sentence contains a single subject and a single verb. You cannot break the sentence at any point and come up with two other simple sentences.

Singular   Term used to distinguish a noun, pronoun, or verb that refers to one person, place, or thing from a noun, pronoun, or verb that refers to more than one.

Smileys   Also known as *emoticons*. A code of punctuation marks used in informal e-mail messages to express emotional cues for text. The symbols resemble facial expressions; for example, :-) is a happy smiley.

Snail-mail   Traditional paper-based letters sent through the U.S. postal system.

Spewing   Posting a large number of articles on the same subject and cross-posting to a number of newsgroups.

Style   Sum of choices, both conscious and unconscious, that a person makes while writing. These choices include words, structure and length of sentences and paragraphs, use of emphatic devices, and so on. The best style is one that is clear and concise.

Subject   Part of a sentence about which something is said. The word or group of words in a sentence that represents what person, place, thing, or idea the sentence is about. <u>Money</u> *talks*.

Subject line   Line in an e-mail message that appears in the recipient's incoming mailbox listing.

Suffix   Group of letters added to the end of a word to form a new word or to alter the word's meaning. For example, the suffix *-ion* can be added to *compress* to form *compression*.

Tense The property of verbs that denotes the time frame of an action. There are three primary tenses in English: *present tense, past tense,* and *future tense.*

To line Line in which e-mail addresses are entered. This specifies the destination of an e-mail message.

Tone Effect produced by a writer's style. It reflects the writer's attitude toward the subject and the reader. Tone can be personal or impersonal, friendly or distant, warm and engaging, or cold and abrupt.

Transition Word or phrase that connects ideas and shows how they are related. Transitions are used between sentences and paragraphs to make writing smoother. Transitions create a point of reference for readers to see how the writing is organized and where it is heading. For example, *additionally, however, accordingly, incidentally, generally, for instance,* and *in conclusion* are all transitions.

Verb Part of a sentence that expresses action or state of being and indicates the time of action or being. *We <u>studied</u> our network options for two weeks.*

Voice Relationship between the actor (subject) and the action (verb) taking place in a sentence. See *active voice* and *passive voice.*

Weasel words See *hedging.*

Word wrap Feature of a text editor that causes text to move to the next line when the current line is full.

Wordy phrase Phrase that uses too many words to express an idea. Wordy phrases often include redundancies, such as *absolutely perfect.*

Appendix

CONVENTIONS FOR POSTING ON THE INTERNET

The Internet is a patchwork quilt of more than 13,000 networks connecting over 15 million people. It includes access to a network news service, which is a distributed bulletin board system with thousands of online discussions covering every topic imaginable. People linked to these public forums participate by sending messages that are similar to e-mail messages. If your network is connected to the Internet, chances are you can participate in network news. While the techniques for writing these messages are similar to those for writing e-mail, several conventions for participating in this public forum are unique. This appendix explains the most common conventions for posting messages to the Internet's network news.

WHAT IS NETWORK NEWS?

Network news on the Internet is delivered via the UNIX-based network known as USENET. USENET is not actually part of the Internet, but is widely available because so many systems on the Internet run UNIX. Each USENET site collects and sends information to other sites, adding new information each time. In this way articles are propagated throughout the network usually within twenty-four hours. USENET discussions are called **newsgroups**. Each newsgroup focuses on a particular topic and contains articles (messages) related to that topic that are posted (sent) by individuals.

The most common way to participate in newsgroup discussions is to use one of the many news reader programs available. These programs let you read and post articles as well as select and organize which newsgroups you want to participate in. Some e-mail systems also let you post articles.

FOLLOW BASIC POSTING NETIQUETTE

Before you start posting articles to newsgroups, you need to understand some basic conventions. In USENET news there are files that are posted with the name FAQ, which is an acronym for frequently asked questions. You can find helpful FAQs on using USENET news in the *newsgroups news.answers, news.newusers.questions,* and *news.announce.newusers.* Here are some basic posting netiquette guidelines to keep in mind before you post an article.

- Read some postings and the FAQs for the newsgroup in which you want to post an article to get a feel for that newsgroup.
- Be considerate of network resources. Your individual postings might not seem like much, but remember you are one of many posting messages. Don't post the same article more than once in the same newsgroup. The default life span for a posted article is normally 7 to 21 days, after which time it is deleted.
- Don't post to the whole network articles that are only of local interest. Few people outside you local area will care that you're selling your car. See if there is an appropriate, geographically limited newsgroup in which to post such an article. For example, newsgroups ending in *.ba* are for the San Francisco bay area, and newsgroups ending in *.ne* are for the New England area.

- Don't forget that anyone can read your posted article. Most Internet newsgroups have thousands of **lurkers**, people who read but never post articles. You never know who is among them. It could be your boss.

- Keep your signature concise. Long signatures files are definitely frowned upon. Don't include elaborate graphics in your signature when posting. Both waste network resources. See Chapter 8 for more information on signature files.

- Cancel an article as quickly as possible if you discover that an article you posted has errors. Even though some people might have already read the incorrect version of your article, the sooner you cancel it the better.

- Avoid flame wars. Flames that have gone on for years are referred to as **holy wars.** One on-going holy war deals with the question of whether the PC or the Mac is better.

- Don't spew. **Spewing** is posting a large number of articles on the same subject and cross-posting to a number of newsgroups. **Cross-posting** means posting the same article to more than one newsgroup.

- Don't blather. **Blathering** is posting an article that doesn't get to the point. Blatherers are just bad writers who write screenfuls of text that could be reduced to a sentence or two. Blatherers responding to an article will include the entire article in their reply rather than edit it to make a point.

- Don't be a net weenie. **Net weenies** enjoy insulting other users by posting flames of any kind, from spelling and grammar criticisms to just plain nasty messages. They fan the flames of holy wars and attack anyone recommending that they take their discussion to e-mail.

- Don't rely on net saints for answers you can easily find yourself. **Net saints** are experienced Internet users willing to share their knowledge with newcomers. If you can't find the answer, ask your host system administrator before posting the question.

■ Don't post an article when you can't get in touch with a person by e-mail. Posting an article sends it to thousands of systems throughout the world. It's inconsiderate to clutter up the network with messages of such limited interest.

WHEN TO SEND E-MAIL RATHER THAN POSTING AN ARTICLE

Just because you're in a public forum doesn't mean you need to post articles publicly to participate. An article lists the e-mail address of the person posting it, so you can respond privately. Most news reader programs let you send e-mail directly to the person posting the article. Here are some guidelines on when to send an e-mail message rather than posting an article.

■ Send an e-mail message rather than post an article when your message is directed to one person; for example, if you want to thank another user.

■ Don't post an article that points out spelling and grammar mistakes you have discovered in a posted article. If you must comment on a mistake, send the author an e-mail message. Keep in mind that, for many on the Internet, English is a second language.

■ Respond to articles that call for yes or no votes via e-mail to the author instead of posting your votes.

TIPS FOR WRITING ARTICLES

Writing an article is similar to writing an e-mail message; however, some unique conventions are observed in article writing. Here are some guidelines to keep in mind as you write an article.

■ Keep your article lines under 80 characters—under 72 if possible.

- Don't use justified alignment in your articles. Besides being harder to read, justified text can cause problems for different terminals. Use a ragged right margin.

- Don't use special characters or control characters in a posting—most of them won't work for most readers. In fact, the space character is about the only one you can be sure will work consistently.

- Be careful when you refer to other articles. Refer to articles by message ID, not by article number. The position of articles varies from system to system.

- Don't use filler lines if a news system rejects your follow-up article because it contains more quoted lines than new text. If, after you edit the original article, you find you are quoting more than you are writing, change the character used to identify the quotation.

- If you post an article that elicits information or opinions, summarize your findings so that others can benefit. It's common for people to ask for replies to an article, then summarize and post the results. This means taking all the responses received and editing them (stripping headers and duplicate information) into a single article and posting the short summary to the original newsgroup. When possible, credit the people who have replied.

  Note: Most news reader programs support a feature known as a **kill file,** also known as the **bozo filter,** which allows you to screen out postings by a particular user or on a particular subject.

FOLLOW THE NEWSGROUP'S RULES

Different newsgroups have different rules. Know the rules for the forum in which you're participating. FAQs are usually available in most newsgroups that have special rules. Here are some rules common to the most popular newsgroups.

- Don't post messages in newsgroups reserved for files or other specific purposes. For example, *news.newusers.questions* is intended for queries, *alt.binaries.pictures* is only for graphics files, *rec.humor* is only for jokes, and *misc.wanted* is for want ads. Discussions for newsgroups designated for a specific purpose belong in a similarly named newsgroup that ends with extension *.d*.

- Encrypt potentially offensive messages with rot-13. Most USENET news readers include a built-in rot-13 command. Encrypting a message forces the reader to make a deliberate effort to read the article. This way it is harder to offend readers. Rot-13 is most often used on jokes that could be considered offensive.

- Include the word *spoiler* in the subject line to notify users that a posting contains information that will reveal a part of a book or movie.

- Test your article postings by posting a few to the *misc.test* newsgroup, which is used for that purpose.

WHAT CAN AND CAN'T BE POSTED

All opinions or statements made in a posted article should be taken as the opinions of the person who wrote the article. They don't represent the opinions of that person's employer, the owner of the computer system from which the article was posted, or anyone involved with the networks that make up the Internet. The following list briefly summarizes what are considered acceptable and unacceptable postings.

- Post announcements of professional products or services that will be of overall benefit to readers on the Internet. Post to the appropriate newsgroup, *comp.newprod*—don't post to a general-purpose newsgroup such as *misc.misc*. Clearly mark your article as a product announcement in the subject line. Don't repeat a product announcement. Stick to technical facts and avoid advertising hype. Inappropriate announcements or articles violating this policy are usually rejected.

- Don't post private e-mail correspondence without the permission of the author of the article. Under copyright statutes, the author of the e-mail message possesses a copyright on material that he or she wrote.

- Don't post instructions on how to perform an illegal act, such as how to obtain cable TV service illegally. You are responsible for any articles you post.

- Post only short extracts of a copyrighted work for purposes of criticism. Reproduction in whole is strictly and explicitly forbidden by U.S. and international copyright law.

- Most newsgroups will not accept announcements regarding current news events. If you want to discuss an event, use the *misc.headlines* newsgroup.

Index